Battleground Europe

SWORD BEACH

Battleground Europe

SWORD BEACH

3RD BRITISH INFANTRY DIVISION'S BATTLE FOR
THE NORMANDY BEACHHEAD

6 June – 10 June 1944

Tim Kilvert-Jones

LEO COOPER

Published by
LEO COOPER
an imprint of
Pen & Sword Books Limited
47 Church Street, Barnsley, South Yorkshire S70 2AS
Copyright © Tim Kilvert-Jones 2001

ISBN 0 85052 673 6

A CIP record of this book is available
from the British Library

Printed in the United Kingdom by
CPI UK

CPI UK is the parent company of
Redwood Books Limited
Trowbridge, Wiltshire

*For up-to-date information on other titles produced under the Leo Cooper
imprint, please telephone or write to:*
Pen & Sword Books Ltd, FREEPOST SF5, 47 Church Street
Barnsley, South Yorkshire S70 2BR
Telephone 01226 734222

CONTENTS

IN MEMORIAM

This book is dedicated to the memory of Colonel Eric T. Lummis, the Suffolk Regiment, veteran of D-Day, noted Regimental officer, and historian. Eric was also a respected friend to several generations of young British Army officers who had the benefit of being taught about the realities of war by this quiet, truly professional soldier, and gentleman.

COLONEL ERIC T. LUMMIS

DIED ON 11TH JUNE 1999, AGED 79.

His Majesty King George VI arrives on the Normandy beaches.
Bob Lilley via Bob Oates

FOREWORD

by

LIEUTENANT-GENERAL SIR MICHAEL JACKSON CB

Former General Officer Commanding
3rd Division

This book provides a valuable tool for all students of war. The author sets the scene for the great drama of Sword Beach and the thrust for Caen, with the broad canvas of D-Day as the backdrop. The work then guides the reader through the complexities of the battles from the beachhead to William the Conqueror's medieval capital astride the River Orne.

This work highlights the realities of command at the operational and tactical levels where decisions – even to this day – are made more frequently with incomplete intelligence, rather than the perfect situational awareness that hindsight allows us. The story of 3rd British Division in Normandy is typical of many Commonwealth infantry divisions committed to battle in the wider struggle to destroy Hitler's European tyranny. The young men who were to bear the brunt of this bloody struggle were drawn from the shires of the United Kingdom and were committed — many men for the first time – to battle in one of the most difficult, complex, and historically significant campaigns in the history of Europe. Their courage, will, and sacrifice contributed to the shattering of German power in France and ultimately, in the course of ten months, throughout Western Europe.

The study of the Normandy campaign remains an important component in the understanding of that profoundly transformative, hugely destructive conflict, that provides historians, students, and warriors with such a rich tapestry of lessons and insights into the realities of total war. The recommended stands in this book give an excellent snap-shot of the five bloody weeks of attrition fought between the men of 3rd British Infantry Division and their ruthless and highly effective foes in the Wehrmacht and Waffen-SS. On D-Day confusion would reign on Sword Beach, where landing schedules slipped and succeeding waves of assault craft piled a jumble of men and vehicles at the water's edge. Even so, the leading troops in Sword sector were off the beach within an hour of landing and by dark had joined up with the forces of the British 6th Airborne

Division astride the Orne and pushed south to within a few miles of the city of Caen. British and Canadian forces failed to seize Caen on D-Day in part because the Germans threw the weight of their available reserves, and the only armored division to hand, into the defense of the city.

D-Day remains one of the epic assaults of history, a "mighty endeavor," as President Franklin D. Roosevelt described it to the American people, "to preserve ... our civilization and to set free a suffering humanity." As with his Omaha Beach edition in this series, the author has succeeded in bringing to life the realities of war, the complexities of command and control and the challenges of coalition operations against a tough resolute enemy who has not forgotten how to fight or how to die.

Tim Kilvert-Jones – formerly a principal staff officer in 3rd Division and the trainer of the divisional staff in Headquarters 3rd Division during its relocation from Germany back to Tidworth under my predecessor's command – has analyzed the operations and tactics that defined the conduct of the battle for Caen, the pivot in the Allied strategy for the liberation of France. The author has presented incisive portraits of the leaders, soldiers, sailors and airmen on both sides of this climactic battle. The ambiguities of the struggle, the opportunities seized or missed, are all examined within a structure that allows the reader to get the very most out of a visit to this historic field of battle. I commend this work to all students, historians, and instructors in the art of war.

Lieutenant General
Sir Michael Jackson CB

INTRODUCTION

Understanding Historic Battlefields

Professor Sir Michael Howard once described three general guidelines for the effective study of military history. He suggested that it should be studied firstly in depth, to get beneath the historian's imposed pattern of seeming orderliness and to try and understand what war is really like, in effect to get an idea of the confused nature of fighting. Secondly, it should be studied in breadth so that the development of war over a long period can be understood. Thirdly, it should be studied in context to appreciate the political, social, and economic factors that exercise important influences on the military part of the equation. The **Battleground Europe** series has been designed to meet his demanding requirements.

The focus of the guidebook will be on one relatively short period during the momentous, but bloody events in Normandy in the mid-20th century, the assault by a joint military force from the United Kingdom on a German defended and fortified sector of the Normandy coastline from 6 June to 10 July 1944.

An appreciation of the military framework behind the operations of 1st British Corps in Sword sector on 6th June 1944 is a fundamental necessity. In order to appreciate the scale of this battlefield and the significance of the great sacrifice made by so many young men in the assault divisions of June 1944, it is essential to visualize the whole 'canvas' of Operation Neptune-Overlord. To that end Chapter 1 will provide sufficient explanation for the reader to fit the more personal accounts of a single division's battles into what Winston Churchill described thus: 'this vast operation is undoubtedly the most complicated and difficult that has ever occurred.'

The specific combat actions that are discussed in this book occurred at the tactical level. The tactical level of war is concerned with the conduct of battles and engagements; these normally unfold within a sequence of major operations. Above this level of military activity lies the operational level of conflict. This level provides the gearing between national political and military strategy and all tactical activities in a theater of operations. It is at the operational level that military resources are directed to achieve the campaign objectives, or end-state. Throughout the Northwest European Campaign, the operational commander was the American General Dwight D.

Eisenhower, the Supreme Allied Commander. Eisenhower arrived in London in January 1944 to take up an appointment that would influence the very conduct of the Anglo-American effort against Germany. He was not operating in a vacuum. Eisenhower received strategic guidance from the political leaders of the western powers principally President Roosevelt of the United States and Prime Minister Winston Churchill in Britain. Military direction was then issued by either the Joint Chiefs, or via the national military strategic authorities; in Washington D.C. General George Marshall spoke for the President, while in London, Field Marshal Sir Alan Brooke (Chief of the Imperial General Staff and Chairman of the Chiefs-of-Staff Committee) spoke for Churchill.

Eisenhower was ably supported by a multi-national staff and most notably by the preliminary planning carried out under the direction of a British officer, Lieutenant General Sir Frederick E. Morgan, Chief of Staff to the as yet unnamed Supreme Allied Commander. It was Morgan's efforts and breadth of vision that provided so much of the planning framework for the subsequent Commonwealth and American victory on D-Day.

D-Day in Perspective

D-Day was the greatest combined amphibious assault the world has yet seen. It was a staggering feat of planning and synchronized military action. On that day a total of 156,205 men, 3,000 guns, 1,500 tanks and 15,000 other assorted vehicles landed in Normandy across the assault beaches or by glider and parachute onto the fields of France. In all, eight allied divisions were put ashore. It was and still is an astonishing achievement. These forces then pressed back the remnants

Camouflaged vehicles lining the roadway of an English south coast village in the weeks leading up to D-Day.

of the German coastal defense units, already battered by air and naval bombardment and then bloodied at close quarters on 6 June. By 2 July the Allied Expeditionary Force had deposited 1,000,000 men ashore including twenty-four divisions at a cost of 60,770 casualties (8,975 were killed). This extraordinary summary of achievement belies the very real fear, exhilaration, cost, and horror endured by those men and women touched by this climactic battle.

On 6 June 1944 disaster would only really threaten the Allies at Omaha Beach. Here the V US Corps launched its Rangers, elements of the 29th 'Blue and Gray' Division under command of the veteran 'Big Red One' (1st Division), in a frontal assault against a natural, well defended, fortress between Pointe du Hoc and St. Honorine. That the operation was to prove successful is a testament to the undaunted courage and small unit leadership of so many young men throughout the Omaha assault force. Their story can be found in the *Omaha Beach* book from this series. Another related title in this series is Carl Shilleto's *Pegasus Bridge/Merville Battery*. The valiant glider force that captured the bridges over the Orne were dependent for their overall success and survival on a timely link-up and relief by troops coming ashore on Sword Beach. On that beach the assault battalions from 8 Infantry Brigade were to suffer localized slaughter disproportionate to the rest of the division as individual boat sections and companies beached into prepared killing areas or directly under the guns of German strongpoints.

In the past the story of the 3rd Division in Normandy has had an inappropriately mixed press. This has been largely due to the adverse criticisms written by the Australian war reporter Chester Wilmot and General Sir David Belcham in their respective books *The Struggle For Europe* and *Victory in Normandy*. A great many writers have followed their baleful influence since these works were first published in 1951 and 1981 and few have thought to challenge them until more recently. Wilmot criticized the division for a lack of drive and a loss of momentum on D-Day caused – as he put it – by being over-trained for the assault rather than focused on the exploitation to Caen. Belcham, the Brigadier General Staff (Operations) of 21 Army Group wrote 'The record of 3rd British Division is the most disappointing of all the assaulting sections... A more dynamic formation would not have dug in at Hermanville but would have devised a plan to outflank the enemy at Periers.' In retrospect these criticisms are largely ill-founded and misconceived. This book will guide the reader and battlefield explorer over the complex terrain and show how enemy action, Clausewitzian friction – an eternal constant in any conflict – and the environment can all play a crucial part in constraining the best devised plans of war. As Colonel Bill Friedman of the 16th Regimental Combat Team landing at Omaha Beach stated after surviving three amphibious assaults against occupied Europe and North Africa:

Once launched this kind of operation is totally out of the hands of higher level commanders... Regardless of the planning, an opposed landing is chaos incarnate. It must be dealt with as such.

Studying Sword Sector using this guide

The three recommended sequential tours of Sword sector can be completed within a day if transport is used, to move between the locations. In this guide the visitor is directed to three sites, or locations, where actions took place – these are referred to as STANDS.

STAND A is located at the seafront town of La Breche d'Hermanville where the landings are described, helping the reader to visualize and relive the events of 6 June 1944.

STAND B is situated on the German bunker system which was code-named 'Hillman' by the Allies. Here the attack on this strongpoint by 1 Suffolks is described in detail.

STAND C forms a vantage point on Periers Ridge to examine the only armoured German counter attack against the beaches on D Day by the elements of 21st Panzer Division.

Each tour is accompanied by a historical account; these accounts should be used as background material to the more poignant study of the ground, the memorials and the personal memories of the men who fought in Sword sector. In addition to these suggested tours, this book provides the reader with selected recommendations for visits to associated sites of general interest within the Lodgment Area. Today, there is no shortage of private museums and memorials competing, along with the more significant national and regional collections, for the visitors' attention and revenue.

You may wish to intersperse studies of the battlefield with visits to appropriate museums in Caen, Ouistreham, Benouville and Bayeux.

D-Day and the Battle for Normandy remain amongst the most fascinating and accessible European military campaigns in the long, painful history of human conflict. Since the end of the Second World War, the region's military history has attracted a broad range of pilgrims. The veterans and their families have been frequent, if unwitting companions to historians and soldiers studying this

The French seaside resort of Colleville-sur-Orne. A few years on and this area would be designated 'Queen Beach' for the Normandy Landings.

momentous campaign.

Whether you will be playing on the beautiful beaches, or touring across the open fields beyond the dunes into the bocage, you cannot avoid the evidence of great sacrifice and terrible loss that surrounds this now beautiful, tranquil and ancient region of France. Nor should the visitor ignore the region's broader tapestry of history and culture. The quiet villages, verdant countryside, dramatic castles, memorials and museums present physical evidence of an Anglo-Saxon, Viking, Norman, French, and English heritage. That dynamic mélange of cultures is characterized by an inscription on the Commonwealth Memorial to the Missing in Bayeux. It reads:

We, once conquered by William, have now set free the Conqueror's Native land.

Maps

Michelin maps are an excellent and essential aid to navigation in Normandy. These maps are a useful start point and can usually be obtained from most well stocked bookshops in France and Britain and on the cross Channel ferries. In the United States they can be obtained from the Institute Geographique National (IGN) distributor at:

Map Link Inc.   or   In Europe IGN can be contacted at:
Map Distributors   ESPACE IGN
30 South La Patera Lane   107, rue la Boetie
Unit#5   75008 Paris
Santa Barbara   France
California 93117   E Mail: www.ign.fr
Tel: (I) (805) 692 6777
Fax: (1) (805) 692 6787

Colville-Plage pre-war. Soon to be in the thick of the fighting on 6 June 1944.

Recommended Maps

Carte Topographique. Institute Geographique National (IGN) Serie Verte Number 6: Cherbourg-Caen 1:100,000. If visits will be made to the eastern extremities of the invasion area then IGN map Number 7 will also be required. This map covers an area from Ouistreham in the west, across the Orne River and its ship canal, where Pegasus Bridge can be found, and so onto the northeast, Merville Battery and beyond.

Other useful maps include Michelin's map Number 54 Normandie in the 1:200,000 series, which covers the whole invasion area, but at a considerably smaller scale.

The serious student or walker may also acquire appropriate maps from the IGN 1:50,000 series in order to find the more obscure routes through the region. These are, however, no longer in print.

A more useful 1: 25,000 series is now available. These maps are the IGN Serie Bleue. This series has been arranged in a wonderfully logical French manner, with all maps the same size and shape. There are a small number of maps that are exceptions to this rule including map number 1512 E, Caen; this larger than normal map covers an area that includes both Juno and Sword Beaches. The eastern boundary runs north south to the east of the river Orne and cuts through the 6th

Airborne sector. The southern boundary runs between the Odon and Hill 112. A new 1:25,000 series entitled La Carte de Randonnee is also available with Caen 1612 OT covering the Jun, Sword, Pegasus Bridge and Merville Battery locations in superb clarity.

Military students are also advised to obtain copies of the excellent French military map series. These maps are available through official map acquisition processes within formation headquarters.

Copies of original Allied planning and battle maps for Neptune-Overlord are now available from the Imperial War Museum, London, for a fee.

ACKNOWLEDGEMENTS

In the research for this book I had the honour and privilege of interviewing a number of those very special veterans from 3rd Division who landed at Sword Beach. I owe my gratitude to every one of these venerable gentlemen who gave so much of their youth and souls in the name of freedom and the service of their nation. We owe them all so very much.

I owe particular thanks to the late Colonel Eric Lummis of the Suffolk Regiment, a true gentleman, warrior, and historian in his own right. He opened my eyes to the realities of a battle that has been simplified and misjudged by several senior officers and historians over time. His dedicated research into the events surrounding 3rd Division's actions in Normandy provided an essential component in the writing of this book.

I also wish to thank Evan Davies for his constructive observations and detailed knowledge of Normandy. Kenneth Fortune, President of REEP Inc. the premier United States military studies Staff Ride Corporation for his support, and Dr. Russell Hart, senior Lecturer in the Department of History at Ohio State University. Dr. Hart gave me full access to his eminent but as yet unpublished dissertation on the battle for Normandy. I am also grateful to Richard Harris, a Normandy veteran of the Suffolk Regiment who very kindly granted me permission to quote from his privately published accounts 50 Years On and The Battle for Chateau de la Londe.

The story of 3rd Division would be incomplete without the contribution of Sir Robin Dunn. As a Battery Commander in 7th Field Regiment Royal Artillery his insights and memories of the battle are critical to any understanding of the opportunities won and lost by the 'Iron Division'.

I must also thank in retrospect the late Colonel Hans von Luck, commander of the 125th Panzer Grenadier Regiment, 21st Panzer Division. He enlightened the author and generations of other NATO officers on a series of now legendary Normandy Staff Rides with his sophisticated analysis of his own experiences in Normandy. Hans was a professional, dedicated warrior whose insights were enriching, forthright and thoughtful.

My wife Louise and our children, Edward, Victoria and Hugo must also be thanked for their patience and tolerance of a husband and father too often confined to his study to meet his publishers' deadline.

Colonel Hans Ulrich von Luck.

Any errors or lack of acknowledgement are the author's fault alone. This book has been written in honour of the veterans who fought in Normandy and for whom there can have been few greater tests than crossing the fire-raked sands or pushing inland against the coastal defence fortifications and the 21st Panzer Division on June 6th, 1944. Those brave men were a very long way from their homes across the Channel on D-Day.

TD Kilvert-Jones
Fairfax, Virginia, USA, June 2001
Tkilve5070@aol.com

We few, we happy few, we band of brothers;
For he today that sheds his blood with me
Shall be my brother; be he ne'er so vile
This day shall gentle his condition.
And gentlemen in England, now a-bed
Shall think themselves accursed they were not here,
And hold their manhoods cheap whiles any speaks
That fought with us upon Saint Crispin's day.

SHAKESPEARE
King Henry V

16

Chapter One

GERMANY'S SECOND FRONT

By the winter of 1943 the Germans were already engaged in a multi-front war. On the Russian Front the finest units of the Wehrmacht and Waffen SS were being consumed at an appalling rate. In the Mediterranean the Axis powers had been defeated in North Africa, an Anglo-American expeditionary force had conquered Sicily and the mainland of Italy had now been invaded. In the skies over Germany an air war of extraordinary proportions was also consuming manpower and industrial production capacity as losses of aircraft and ground defenses climbed. In an effort to stem the devastating tide of day and night area bombing by the Allied bomber fleets, the Germans relocated fighter wings and air defense systems to protect the Fatherland at the cost of other fronts. The German air defense system (including searchlight units, gun crews, and radar centres) had absorbed 900,000

Defending the Reich from night and day bombing raids was absorbing large numbers of men, armaments and munitions.

men alone. All these assets were being employed well away from what was to be the decisive 'Second Front.'

Defending the Reich: Fortress Europe

In December 1941 Adolf Hitler ordered his national military command headquarters, the Oberkommando der Wehrmacht (OKW), to plan,

> 'The construction of a new West Wall to assure protection of the Arctic, North Sea and Atlantic coasts against any landing operation of very considerable strength with the employment of the smallest number of static forces.'

On 23 March 1942, with the Third Reich at the peak of its success, he went on to issue his Führer Directive Number 40. This directive set down the detailed defensive responsibilities for the operational commanders in the West. It stated:

> 'The coastline of Europe will, in the coming months, be exposed to the danger of the enemy landing in force... Even enemy landings with limited objectives can interfere seriously with our own plans if they result in the enemy gaining any kind of foothold on the coast... Enemy forces that have landed must be destroyed or thrown back into the sea by immediate counterattack.'

Ironically three days after he had signed this directive the British mounted the highly successful – though costly – raid on the port and dry dock facilities at St. Nazaire. The raid was so effective that the 'Normandie' dry dock (destroyed by the explosive-laden HMS *Campbletown*) was inoperable for the rest of the war. Within five months, on 19 August, the German defences were further probed by Operation JUBILEE, the disastrous raid at Dieppe. This operation was a frontal assault on a partly fortified harbour. The German defenders used their limited fortifications and counter-attack troops to devastating effect. After nine hours the remnants of the Anglo-Canadian force withdrew leaving behind 3,658 men out of the 5,100 troops who had landed. One thousand men had been killed and the remainder was wounded, missing, or taken prisoner. The Germans had suffered 300 casualties.

The costly experience at Dieppe was to provide diverse lessons that would be fundamental to the subsequent successful landings in North Africa, Sicily in 1943, and in Normandy one year later. Each side drew very different conclusions from the disaster. For the Germans a greater emphasis on fixed fortifications became the order of the day. For the Allies a more detailed analysis produced far reaching lessons-learned

Valuable experience in amphibious landing techniques were gained through Operations TORCH (Tunisia) and HUSKY (Sicily).

General Patton surveys the beaches following the successful landings in Sicily.

that would ultimately support NEPTUNE-OVERLORD. For the most part, the German newspaper headlines in late August 1942 illustrated the Führer's sentiments on JUBILEE: 'Catastrophic Defeat a Setback to Invasion...What does Stalin say about this Disaster to Churchill's Invasion?' For the Reich the Allied disaster provided valuable propaganda material and a reassurance that lightly held fortified defences could repel enemy amphibious assaults. The Germans certainly viewed the Anglo-Canadian operation as an amateurish undertaking. In truth, it had been.

Work on the West Wall (also known as the Atlantic Wall, a component of Fortress Europe) now began in earnest amid a blaze of propaganda. The focus of effort was on the major ports (the evident target of enemy raids and any future invasion) and then on vulnerable coastal areas, such as the Pas de Calais, Hook of Holland and the Gironde estuary. The Germans had once again forgotten their own history; it was Frederick the Great of Prussia who had stated, 'He who defends everything, defends nothing.' In reality, what emerged was a loose necklace of powerful fortresses such as Calais and Cherbourg,

Workers of the Todt Organization constructing a massive bunker on the French coastline. Reinforcing steel rods are being put in place prior to the pouring of concrete.

interconnected by weak outposts and routine patrol activities spread over 2,400 miles of coastline. Inflexible dogma and self-delusion had replaced effective critical analysis of the threat now gathering strength across the Channel.

The Germans were also hampered by shortages of defensive materials such as concrete, mines, adequate weapons, fighting men and labor. By 1943 the war in the East was draining the Reich's increasingly limited resources and this was now impacting on every front. The aging Field Marshal Gerd Von Rundstedt, Commander-in-Chief West (OB West), identified the serious manpower shortfall. He reported in October 1943, that the existing West Wall could be covered but not fully defended. Yet he also recognized the utility of the Wall as a propaganda tool and, to a lesser extent, the military value of Hitler's port-city fortress policy. That policy would actually lead to the denial or destruction of the principal French ports in the face of the Allied advance for several months after D-Day and impact on the Allied line of operations for the rest of 1944. However, Von Rundstedt went on to note that:

> 'A rigid German defense (is) impossible there for any length of time, the outcome of the battle must depend on the use of a mobile and armoured reserve... the best that might be hoped for [is] that it might hold up an attack for twenty four hours, but any resolute assault [is] bound to make a breakthrough anywhere along it in a day at most. And once through all the rest could be taken from the rear...'

Generalfeldmarschall Gerd von Rundstedt

Führer Directive Number 51

On 3 November 1943 Hitler issued one of the half dozen of his most significant directives of the war. Führer Directive Number 51 specified the tasks required of OB West to create an effective bastion against an Anglo-American landing. The Directive stated:

> '...If the enemy here succeeds in penetrating our defences on a wide front, consequences of staggering proportions will follow within a short time. All signs point to an offensive in the Western Front no later than spring, and perhaps earlier.'

For that reason I can no longer justify the further weakening of the West in favor of other theatres of war. I have therefore decided to strengthen the defences in the West, particularly at places from which we shall launch our long-range war against England. For those are the very points at which the enemy must and will attack: there – unless all indications are misleading – will be fought the decisive invasion battle.

Hitler went on to issue specific tasks to the Army, Luftwaffe, Navy, and SS and closed with a warning:

'All authorities will guard against wasting time and energy in useless jurisdictional squabbles, and will direct all their efforts toward strengthening our defensive and offensive power.'

Adolf Hitler, a dictator in every sense of the word, concerned himself in almost every aspect of the total war being waged by Nazi Germany.

Fortunately for the Allies, Hitler's subordinate component commanders and even individual arms commanders ignored this final demand. That divisive situation would be further exacerbated by his imposition of a complex, contradictory, and ineffective command structure on his forces in the West.

Field Marshal Erwin Rommel in the West: December 1943

By 5 November 1943 Hitler had promulgated his new Directive Number 51 and selected Rommel as his Inspector General of Defences in the West. By the end of that month Rommel had gathered about him a specialist joint staff to support his analysis of the West Wall. He moved from Italy to France with his own Army Group B headquarters and quickly set about a grueling programme of inspections from Denmark to the Spanish border. He focused much of his effort on the most likely areas for the impending invasion: Pas de Calais, the Somme estuary, Normandy – including the Cotentin Peninsula, Brittany, and the Netherlands.

As a result of Rommel's highly critical report and recommendations, Hitler decided to incorporate Army Group B into OB West on 31 December. Rommel now found himself under Von Rundstedt's command, with specific responsibility for anti-invasion plans from the Netherlands and across northern France. His command was divided into the Seventh Army West of the River Orne, and Fifteenth Army to

Feldmarschall **Erwin Rommel applied his brilliant military mind to improving Europe's coastal defences.**

its East, with the 88th Corps in Holland.

Rommel assessed that to have any hope of success 'the enemy must be annihilated before he reaches our main battle line,' therefore 'we must stop him in the water.' Rommel ordered the laying of 200 million mines along the coast to form an initial barrier. Between November 1943 and mid-May 1944 over half a million anti-invasion obstacles were put in place along with a total of 4 million mines. One month before the invasion he was able to report,

> *'I am more confident than ever before. If the British give us just two more weeks, I won't have any more doubt about it.'*

The frenetic preparatory activity throughout Army Group B was a major concern to the Allies. In fact, the Allied planners were so concerned with Rommel's beach defences that they adjusted the preferred time and conditions necessary for the amphibious assault. The seaborne invasion had been initially planned to take place under the cover of darkness, but now it would commence after first light. Better visibility would give the navy a chance to manoeuvre through the increasingly complex and lethal 'forest' of obstacles along the beaches.

German Intelligence Assessments and the
Impact on Defensive Strategy

During early 1944 Rommel would bemoan his lack of knowledge of Allied intentions. He wrote, 'I know nothing for certain about the enemy.' The Allied air forces were effectively preventing most German reconnaissance flights reaching the southern coast of Britain – now densely packed with shipping, men, and materiel. Rommel was strategically blind. His headquarters along with *Fremde Heeres West* (Foreign Armies West), the German military intelligence organization, focused on establishing the strength and intentions of the Anglo-American armies in Britain, was also completely misled by BODYGUARD and the deception operations protecting NEPTUNE-OVERLORD. On 20 March they could do little better than assess that the impending assault would occur 'somewhere between the Pas de Calais and the Loire valley'.

As a result of the complex deception conducted within the BODYGUARD framework of operations, the Germans believed that the Allies had ninety operational divisions plus an additional seven airborne divisions in the UK (double the actual strength). They assessed that twenty of those divisions were poised to land in the first wave – four times the actual strength intended for the D-Day assault. The Germans believed that with so many divisions apparently prepared for the forthcoming invasion, the Anglo-American forces would be able to mount two expeditions in rapid succession, probably in the Pas de Calais and one other location. German assessments of this fictitious Allied capability and intent were further manipulated and reinforced by the information passed back to the Reich by German 'turned' agents in Britain, most notably agent GARBO.

The Abwehr (German Military Intelligence) staff in Spain had recruited GARBO, or rather Juan Pujol Garcia, as a potential agent for operations in Britain. By the time Pujol was deployed to southern England in 1942 he had already been 'turned.' As a controlled double agent he established a fictitious network of twenty-seven additional 'sources' located across the southern counties. GARBO then passed an intricate web of deception back to his Abwehr controller, Karl Erich Kuhlenthal, in Spain. Kuhlenthal was so impressed with the information that he retransmitted it to his headquarters in Berlin. The Abwehr informed GARBO:

> *'Your activity and that of your informants gave us a perfect idea of what is taking place over there. These reports...have an incalculable value.'*

Ironically the Germans were to decorate Pujol for his services to their war effort with the Iron Cross on 17 June 1944. Within months the Director General of MI5 would also award him with an MBE for his contribution to both the Bodyguard operation and the fixing of the German Fifteenth Army in the Pas de Calais.

Blind and misled, Rommel still managed to analyze the threat and conceive of a credible defensive strategy that with hindsight and evidence from Omaha Beach appears to have had the best chance of actually defeating or disrupting the invasion. Unfortunately for the dynamic and energetic commander of Army Group B, he lacked the resources to convert theory in to reality. In mid-May 1944 Oberst Oehmichen published a German Seventh Army staff report. He illuminated the shortfalls in defensive preparations in Normandy and compared the state of the coastal defences with Fifteenth Army in the Pas de Calais. Some of his findings would have made disturbing reading for Erwin Rommel:

Defensive Capability	Seventh Army Normandy	Fifteenth Army Calais
Divisional Frontage	40-270 Kms	40 Kms
Mine Density-T mine	440 per Km 30 in the invasion area	
Heavy Guns in Bunkers	27 out of 47 guns	93 out of 132
Fixed Anti-Tank Guns in Bunkers	9 guns all in the open	16 out of 82 under cover
Resistance Nest (WN) Density	1,300 Meters	875 Meters
Anti-Tank Gun Density	12.25 per 10 Kms	22 guns per 10 ms

Any obstacle crossing or expeditionary operation is most vulnerable to counter-attack while the assaulting force is establishing its beachhead. If Rommel could hold the assault divisions on the foreshore and then launch local counter attacks using all available armoured forces, he would stand a good chance of disrupting or defeating the invasion. In Normandy, the German defences would lack any depth and as the commander of 716th Coastal Defence Division described his resistance nests, they were like 'a string of pearls' along the coast. In the absence of effective defences in depth, Rommel would be dependent on reserves – particularly the armoured reserves – from the interior, to crush an Allied lodgment.

Even as late as 1944 there was no doubt of German superiority in armour. The panzers would have a dramatic impact on any landing operation – if they could be positioned in hides close to the likely invasion beaches – an assessment born out by events on D-Day in Sword Sector.

The German armoured Reserves

Following his detailed analysis of the situation, Rommel now sought control of the panzer forces then under command of his higher headquarters at OB West. As a result of his experiences in North Africa, where his Afrika Korps had been under relentless enemy air attacks in the latter phase of the North Africa campaign, Rommel recognized the need to deploy his reserves well forward. This would minimize their exposure to both direct air attacks and the effects of enemy air

The work horse of the Panzer units – PzKpfw IVs of the 2nd Panzer Division move through a French village in 1944.

interdiction around the landing area. Rommel was also at a fundamental disadvantage with the absence of any effective intelligence, even if he gained control of the critical armoured reserves, he would have to disperse these limited resources to cover the most likely invasion areas: from the Pas de Calais through Normandy to the Cotentin. Yet once the direction of the enemy attack had been identified he would still be able to throw the nearest panzer units into battle, if necessary piecemeal. He felt that he could afford to do this because of the qualitative advantage of the German panzers over any Allied fighting vehicle then in service. Individually, there was little doubt that German tanks were superior. They had better armour and carried more powerful weapons and were usually commanded and crewed by experienced veterans. This meant that in most engagements each individual German tank had a qualitative and often a tactical advantage over its numerically superior enemy counterparts.

Once Rommel had codified his strategy for defeating the invasion, he sought the resources to make the concept a reality. He now demanded operational control of the panzer arm in OB West. However, a fundamental disagreement emerged between two divergent doctrinal camps. On the one hand Rommel believed in the forward deployment of the panzers and had some support from Hitler. On the other hand the veteran panzer commanders from the Eastern Front, such as General der Panzertruppen Geyr Von Schweppenburg, supported by Guderian (Inspector General of Panzers) and the aging Von Rundstedt, favored holding the panzer reserves well back from the coast until the enemy's intentions and strength became clear; at that point a well-planned and concentrated counter attack could be launched.

Rommel therefore demanded operational control of all the armoured formations in OB West. This would then allow him site these powerful forces in forward concentration areas close to the likely invasion sites along the coastline. From their hides he would then be able to deploy them promptly and with the shortest exposure to air attack to the invasion front.

Within his concept of operations, Rommel planned to use his nearest panzer divisions as a hasty counter attack force. In June 1944 the 21st Panzer Division would be the nearest armoured formation to the Normandy coast on D-Day. Defeated and incarcerated in Tunisia, North Africa, it was reformed in Rennes, Brittany on 15 July 1943 and equipped with an assortment of captured French vehicles from the 1940 campaign. By June 1944 the Division could boast between its Panzer Regiment 22, Sturmgeschutz (Stug.) Abteilung 200, and Panzer

French Hotchkiss H-39 (*Geschützwagen*) chassis mounting a 105mm howitzer made an effective assault gun and was used to equip the reformed 21st Panzer Division.

Artillerie Regiment 155:

    98 PzKpfw IV (6 were old model Gs)

    6 PzKpfw IIIs

    23 French Somuas

    43 improvised assault guns mounted on French Hotchkiss chassis

    45 Lorraine conversions

This numerically powerful looking force was actually a shadow of its former self when it had fought in Rommel's Afrika Korps. By July 1944 it would once again be shattered after a month of combat: the force would be down to 61 PzKpfw IVs and 32 Hotchkiss guns, and 45 'Lorraines'. On 1 August 1944 the Division would have only 42 PzKpfw IVs left.

While the initial action was being fought to both bolster the coastal defences and destroy localized penetrations, Rommel intended to bring the more distant formations to the battle area to mount further attacks on any weakly held enemy lodgments. Those more distant divisions would need to redeploy to the new front, moving on exterior lines, and probably being harried from the air by Allied fighter bombers operating well within range of the French coast from their British airfields.

This inevitably exposed journey could still prove to be shorter and less dangerous than a move from some inland concentration area designated by the cautious Von Rundstedt, or the traditional cavalry tacticians who wanted to mass their panzer arm before delivering a 'text-book' decisive blow. This traditional approach ignored the inherent strength of Allied air power and the ability of the Anglo-American armies to concentrate artillery and naval gunfire in devastating co-ordinated bombardments. It also fell exactly into place with General Montgomery's assessment of how the German's would conduct the defense. During his briefing, codenamed EXERCISE THUNDERCLAP, to all general officers of the Field Armies at St. Paul's School, London on 7-8 April 1944, Montgomery explained that:

> *'Rommel is likely to hold his mobile divisions back from the coast until he is certain where our main effort is being made. He will concentrate them quickly and strike a hard blow, his static divisions will endeavour to hold on defensively to important ground and act as pivots to counter-attacks...'*

Unfortunately for Rommel, Von Schweppenburg was commanding Panzer Group West, headquartered in Paris close to Von Rundstedt's OB West Headquarters. In 1944 Von Schweppenburg had responsibility for the training of the panzer and panzergrenadier divisions under Von Rundstedt's command. His principal staff was composed entirely of experienced panzer and grenadier officers. From Paris, Geyr also retained an element of operational control over three of the armoured divisions in theatre. These responsibilities were now to bring him into direct contact – and on occasions, conflict – with Rommel.

German Unity of Effort and Unity of Command

Fortunately for the Allies neither German camp won the argument of control over the *Panzertruppen*. Hitler, ever suspicious of his army commanders, actually allowed the debate to impede any form of unified command in the West. He received a series of visitors who lobbied him in favor of one or other solutions. Guderian describes in his memoirs one such visit to gain Hitler's support for the formation of a Front Reserve. The response to this request was a long statistical summary of fortification and mining programs conducted on the West Wall and an endorsement of the 'Rommel Doctrine' that the first forty-eight hours of the invasion would be critical.

Back in France, Rommel was engaged in acrimonious debates with Von Rundstedt over the location of individual divisions, such as their

Feldmarschall Rommel (left), Feldmarschall von Rundstedt (hands on hips) and General Gause pay attention as Oberst Zimmermann makes a point on the map (sensored).

argument over the location of the 2nd Panzer Division astride the River Somme at Abbeville. In such an atmosphere of mistrust, Rommel alternated between bouts of defeatism to absolute confidence. His swings of emotion were noted and briefed to Hitler who finally decided to temporize. North of the River Loire, Rommel (Army Group B) was given command of 2nd, 21st and 116th Panzer Divisions. So in all, Rommel now had thirty-nine infantry and three panzer divisions under his command in June 1944. Of his vital panzer formations, 21st Panzer Division was located near Caen, the coastline that would soon become known as Sword Beach, and the Orne Bridges. 2nd Panzer Division was located in the Pas de Calais, and the 116th was concentrated near Paris.

Hitler left Von Rundstedt in nominal command of Panzer Group West including Panzer Lehr, and 12th SS *Hitler Jugend* in accordance with OKW's recommendation. To add to this complex command structure the 12th SS Panzer and 17th SS Panzergrenadier Divisions along with 1st SS *Leibstandarte* were part of the 1st SS Panzer Corps under SS General 'Sepp' Dietrich. These powerful, elite forces were dispersed between Brussels and Poitiers.

Ironically, in Führer Directive Number 40 of 23 March 1942, entitled Command Organisations on the Coasts, Hitler had stated:

> *'The preparation and execution of defensive operations must unequivocally and unreservedly be concentrated in the hands of one man.'*

It was fortunate for the Allies that Hitler did not follow through and enforce all his directives.

Inevitably, each layer of authority that Hitler imposed on his generals would add new complexities and frictions to the already hardened arteries of command in OB West. To add a final measure of delay to any flexible or responsive decision-making, Hitler demanded that none of the armoured reserves could be deployed without his personal authority. Crucial hours and days would now be lost from midnight on 6 June as the army commanders awaited decisions from their distant Commander-in-Chief. In truth, Hitler had ensured that neither of his Field Marshals in the West would have flexible command over the crucial armoured reserves at the very moment when hours rather than days would be decisive.

Germany's Multiple Front War: the Eastern Front and Normandy

At the strategic level one must recognise and pay tribute to the Soviet contribution to the success of D-Day. In reality the Red Army was grinding the greater part of the German war machine to dust far away from Normandy. In 1943 at the Tehran conference, Stalin had promised to launch an offensive that would fix and disrupt Hitler's ability to switch assets from Russia to France during the critical first month of the build-up in Normandy.

As June progressed, the strategic situation would deteriorate further for the Reich as Hitler became distracted by events in the East and the preparations for the expected Soviet summer offensive codenamed BAGRATION.

OPERATION BAGRATION would annihilate Germany's Army Group Centre between 22-30 June. This Soviet offensive in western Russia had been timed to disrupt German attempts to switch reserves from the Eastern Front to meet the new threat in Normandy. With over 1.7 million men supported by over 4,000 tanks and assault guns, 6,000 aircraft and 26,000 artillery or rocket systems, the Soviet Union shattered the German frontline. Within a week the Third Reich had lost 154,000 men, either killed or taken prisoner. Materiel losses defy imagination; in one week, 2,000 tanks, 10,000 guns and 57,000 vehicles had been destroyed or captured. These losses exceed even those endured at Stalingrad. While Army Group Center was being crushed, Army Group North was being cleaved in two and forced into retreat towards East Prussia and the Baltic States.

This level of attrition puts in perspective the Allied sacrifices on D-Day. Now when the visitor to Normandy stands at La Breche or on the bunkers at Hillman and looks down over Queen White and Red, it is worth pondering the contribution of the Soviets to this particular victory.

The Russian Summer offensive of 1944 smashed through German Army Group Centre. Here some 50,000 German prisoners are being marched through the streets of Moscow. After their passage the road was swilled with disinfectant.

CHAPTER TWO

THE ALLIES PREPARE

Allied Combined Operations: the Second Front

The intelligence preparations for the Second Front had actually commenced in 1941 as part of a general analysis of occupied Europe. In October of that year, Prime Minister Winston Churchill had summoned Lord Louis Mountbatten back from the Fleet to take command of Combined Operations Headquarters. The direction that he received from the Prime Minister was truly inspiring given that British fortunes were at their lowest ebb. Churchill issued him with the following order:

'I now want you to start the preparations for our great counter-invasion of Europe. Unless we can land overwhelming forces and beat the Nazis in battle in France, Hitler will never be defeated. So this must be your prime task. I want you to work out the philosophy of invasion, to land and advance against the enemy. You must collect the most brilliant planners in the three services to help you. You must devise and design new landing craft, appurtenances and appliances and train the three services to act together as a single force in combined operation. All other headquarters in England are engaged on defensive measures; your Headquarters must think only of offense.'

Having taken up the appointment, Mountbatten established a philosophy that would assist both him and his successors in designing the campaign plan for the Second Front. He recognized that the Allies must:

'Firstly be certain of obtaining a firm lodgment at the desired place on the enemy-held coast against all known defences.

'Secondly, to break out of the beachheads while reinforcements of men, vehicles, munitions, and stores continued ceaselessly to follow up the spearhead no matter what the weather conditions during the following weeks.

'And thirdly, at the same time to keep the main enemy forces as far from the landing area by deception and prevent them, when they discovered the deception, from moving reinforcements to the landing area faster than the build-up of the invasion force, by bombing all road and rail communications over a wide area for several months beforehand.'

In comparison to the gloating German response, Lord Louis

Mountbatten's rapidly growing staff at Combined Operations Command drew very different lessons from OPERATION JUBILEE. The British produced a remarkably forthright and very constructive Combined Report on the Dieppe Raid that was signed by Mountbatten himself in October 1942. Lieutenant General Morgan and his staff certainly benefited from the report and its associated lessons learnt. The report stated most significantly:

'The Lesson of Greatest Importance is the need for overwhelming fire support, including close support, during the initial stages of the attack. It is not too much to say that, at present, no standard naval vessel or craft has the necessary qualities or equipment to provide close inshore support. Without such support any assault on the enemy-occupied coast of Europe is more and more likely to fail as the enemy's defenses are extended and improved.'

Ultimately, although the cost was terrible, the experience gained at Dieppe, and then subsequently in North Africa and Sicily would prove essential to Eisenhower's 'Great Crusade.' Mountbatten later assessed that for every casualty suffered at Dieppe the Allies had saved ten men in Normandy.

In April 1943 Lieutenant General Morgan, Chief of Staff to the as yet un-named Supreme Allied Commander (COSSAC), had warned his team,

'the term planning staff has come to have a sinister meaning. It implies the production of nothing but paper. What we must contrive to do somehow is to produce not only paper but action.'

The following month in Washington, Roosevelt and Churchill together with their military advisors agreed to launch an offensive against the Atlantic Wall in 1944. Over the next month COSSAC and the Combined Operations Command completed a highly detailed military appreciation. They concluded at a conference, codenamed RATTLE, that Normandy was the optimal target for the invasion. Roosevelt and Churchill endorsed this at the Quebec Conference (QUADRANT) in August 1943. A provisional date of 1st May 1944 was identified for D-Day under the codename OVERLORD.

Lieutenant General Morgan. Architect of OVERLORD.

One of the foremost deductions in the COSSAC appreciation was that the Allies could not launch the invasion head-on against a fortified

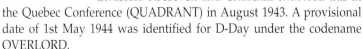

port, nor could they count on capturing such a facility during the critical build-up phase. It was inevitable that once the Allies had shown their hand the Germans would be rushing reinforcements up to the lodgment area to first contain and then destroy the forces in the beachhead. As General Bradley said in his address to the Press on board USS *Augusta* on Saturday evening 3 June 1944:

'You've got to remember that just as soon as we land, this business becomes primarily a business of build-up. For you can almost always force an invasion – but you can't always make it stick.'

The outcome of this decisive race to achieve numerical and materiel superiority would depend on the Allies ability to land, deploy and subsequently supply the combat forces designated for Operation OVERLORD. A port facility would therefore be critical. German intelligence had as yet no knowledge of the artificial, prefabricated Mulberry harbour concept, so in the absence of an alternative, Hitler's fortress-port policy made considerable sense. By denying the Anglo-American forces any substantial dock facilities, Hitler hoped to starve any second front of the necessary logistic resources required to achieve a decisive build-up and concentration of force for a breakout towards the Reich.

In isolation Hitler may have been right. However, Operation NEPTUNE-OVERLORD was the opening stage of a much larger, combined and joint campaign. That campaign would be supported by a remarkable and highly effective deception plan codenamed BODYGUARD designed to tie down many of Hitler's reserves away from the Norman coastline.

Once ashore the Allied armies would be sustained by vast stocks of materiel and while they would be struggling to build-up their combat power in the lodgment area, the combined naval fleets and air forces of Britain and the United States would be supporting and protecting them. The Allied air forces would prove to be particularly effective in disrupting German road, rail and air communications, thereby hampering or delaying the arrival of German reinforcements in the battle area. Rommel had recognized that by 1944 the very nature of war had changed and that even the veteran units from the East were in for a shock. Fritz Bayerlain, the commander of Panzer Lehr, recalled Rommel's prophetic words:

'Our friends from the East cannot imagine what they're in for here. It's not a matter of fanatical hordes to be driven forward in masses against our line, with no regard for casualties and little recourse to tactical craft; here we are facing an enemy who applies all his native

intelligence to the use of his many technical resources, who spares no expenditure of material and whose every operation goes its course as it had been subject of repeated rehearsal. Dash and doggedness no longer make a soldier...'

The Allied Joint and Combined Campaign Plans Evolve

After many debates Churchill and Roosevelt agreed that General Dwight D. Eisenhower should be the Supreme Allied Commander for OVERLORD. Eisenhower was notified on 7 December 1943. Ironically, only five days later in Germany, Hitler appointed Erwin Rommel to establish a new command for the defense of the Atlantic Wall. At the very time that Rommel was making his presence felt along the northwest European coastline, the Allied command team was being appointed and gathered just across the channel on Christmas Eve 1943:

SUPREME COMMADER, ALLIED EXPEDITIONARY FORCES:

General Eisenhower

DEPUTY SUPREME COMMANDER:

Air Chief Marshal, Sir Christian Tedder

COMMANDER IN CHIEF ALLIED NAVAL EXPEDITIONARY FORCES:

Admiral Sir Bertram Ramsay

COMMANDER 21ST ARMY GROUP:

General Sir Bernard Montgomery

Shortly after being appointed, Montgomery analyzed the plan proposed by COSSAC. He quickly identified critical flaws in the concept of operations. General Morgan had designed his plan based on the resources he had been allocated for this mission. Morgan had been working on the assumption that only three divisions could be used in the first assault wave. Montgomery rightly considered this to be too small a force deployed over too narrow a frontage. He recommended, and obtained Eisenhower's support that the assault should be expanded to a five-division operation with four divisions in the follow-up wave. He reasoned that this would increase the chances of success by stretching the German response over a wider area, providing greater security to the lodgment, and facilitating the capture of key objectives, namely the Port of Cherbourg and the road and rail communications hub at Caen.

On 21 January these changes were implemented along with a new target date of 31 May 1944. This delay would be essential if the necessary resources for a substantially larger operation were to be built both in Northern America and Britain and then gathered in the United

Air Chief Marshal Tedder, General Eisenhower and General Sir Bernard Law Montegomery seated, with General Bradley, Admiral Ramsay, Air Chief Marshal Sir Trafford Leigh-Mallory and General Walter Bedell Smith.

Kingdom in time for D-Day. The changes were then integrated into the *Initial Joint Plan* (IJP) dated 2 February 1944.

The decision to expand the scale of NEPTUNE-OVERLORD by extending the landing area to include the Cotentin (Utah Beach) and the Orne (Sword Beach between Lion-sur-Mer and Ouistreham) had a major impact on 3rd Division's plan. To date all 1st Corps and divisional planning and training had been conducted on the assumption that the 3rd Division would assault with two brigades astride in the first wave. The IJP stated otherwise; due to shortfalls in appropriate assault landing craft, and terrain constraints, the 3rd Division was now ordered to prepare for an echeloned assault. General Dempsey, Commander of 2nd Army, is on record that it was done to provide more depth to the attack. But on the basis of the IJP there was no alternative. 2nd Army would be landing with five brigades in the initial assault.

It is true that Sword Beach was only half the width of those beaches used at Bernieres-sur-Mer (Juno) and Le Hamel (Gold). This was because of the constraints imposed by the small cliffs that lie at the western end of Sword Beach and the offshore rock shelves running out to sea that would have prevented landing craft from approaching that section of the beach. At the eastern end of Sword Beach the estuary of the River Orne has created an extensive, shallow fan of sand and silt that further impeded landing craft from closing with and then extracting from this section of the beach.

The IJP also declared that three airborne divisions would be used to secure the flanks and fix German forces in place during the critical and highly vulnerable amphibious landing phase.

The final assault plan divided the land operation into two sectors. In the West the First US Army, under General Omar N. Bradley, would

land three infantry divisions on the beaches codenamed Utah and Omaha. Two American airborne divisions (the 82nd and 101st Airborne) would be dropped or landed in gliders on the western flank to dislocate the German response and thereby assist the amphibious forces ashore. In the east, the 2nd British Army under General Miles Dempsey would land on three beaches, codenamed Gold, Juno and Sword with an infantry division on each. On the eastern flank the British 6th Airborne Division would land by parachute and glider and seize the critical bridges over the River Orne and its canal. This division would also secure the high ground east of the river as a bridgehead for subsequent operations. It was also hoped that these operations would hamper and generally disrupt German deployments from around Caen against the eastern beaches

General Sir Miles Dempsey. 2nd British Army.

(Sword and Juno) during the first critical hours of the invasion. The plan was that the five beaches would then be linked-up by midnight on D-Day. By setting his initial objectives deep, Montgomery wanted to encourage dash and élan amongst his formation commanders. The greater the depth achieved, the less likely the invasion would be stalled on the beaches as had happened at Gallipoli in 1915 and Anzio in 1943.

The final date for mounting the operation and the time for the assault to begin were also critical command decisions for Eisenhower. The land component wanted to land in darkness in the hope of gaining tactical surprise – particularly across the exposed beaches. The navy and air component commanders preferred to mount daylight operations in order to ensure more accurate bombardments of enemy targets. The navy was also concerned that in poor sea conditions the already complex task of controlling the vast fleet of assault craft would be all the more hazardous and difficult in darkness.

As a result of Rommel's deployment of defensive obstacles on the Norman foreshore, Ramsey and Eisenhower agreed on 1st May 1944 that the assault would have to take place three to four hours before high tide, and about ten minutes after sunrise. The night before the landing would require good moonlight to support the accurate drop of the airborne divisions and the bombing strikes. All these conditions could only be met on about three days in each lunar month. The final factor would be the weather itself, and this could not be forecast with any real degree of accuracy too far ahead. As a result of all these complex factors the actual date and time for D-Day could not be decided until nearer the window of opportunity in late May-early June. But if the invasion was not launched then, it would have to be delayed for several weeks before the correct conditions of Moon and tide recurred.

The Joint Campaign: Allied Air Power

By 1944 the Allies had developed an ever-improving joint force capability (the art of operating and exploiting the synergy between separate military services) within a combined (the operations of multinational forces in a coalition or an alliance) environment. On 14 April 1944 the overall direction of Allied strategic forces passed to General Eisenhower. He promptly instructed his British deputy, Air Chief Marshal Arthur Tedder, to act as an intermediary between the various interests of the Allied air commanders in order to create an overall operational plan in support of the forthcoming invasion.

Tedder assisted the Allied effort by shaping, designing and activating a devastating air campaign that would support the expeditionary phase and subsequent land battle in Normandy. With the Allied Expeditionary Air Force under the overall command of Air Chief Marshal Sir Trafford Leigh-Mallory, air forces were assigned to conduct both defensive (force protection) and offensive tasks. To ensure that these were properly integrated within the Neptune Overlord phases, Leigh-Mallory considered that:

> 'The air operations in immediate and direct support of the land battle should be specially co-ordinated and directed. I, therefore, decided to establish a small operational organisation to be known as Advanced Allied Expeditionary Air Force [AEAF]. Under my general direction,

the Commander Advanced AEAF was given the task of directing and coordinating the planning for and operations of such forces of the Ninth Air Force and Second Tactical Air Force as were allotted to him from time to time.'

Amidst fierce argument and bitterness, Tedder and Leigh-Mallory succeeded in achieving a concentration of effort from the Allied air forces that would make a significant contribution to the overall campaign. The Allied air plan for NEPTUNE-OVERLORD stated that the general aim of the Allied air forces would be:

'To attain and maintain an air situation which would assure freedom of action for our Forces without effective interference by enemy air forces and to render air support to our Land and Naval Forces in the achievement of this objective.'

To achieve this aim the following tasks were to be fulfilled in a four-phase air campaign:

Phase 1. The first phase of air operations consisted of air interdiction of enemy naval and air assets in the Channel area, in addition to extensive air reconnaissance operations.

Phase 2. This phase commenced in March 1944 and was known as the preparatory phase. As D-Day approached the combined weight of air operations would fall on targets associated with the invasion. This included the use of heavy bombers to attack fortresses, naval facilities and lines of communication (rail, road and surveillance assets such as coastal radar stations). During this phase two out of three raids were still being conducted away from Normandy to maintain the deception plan.

Phases 3 and 4. These last two phases were designed to support the actual invasion and the subsequent battle for Normandy. The scale of effort was remarkable: fifty-four fighter squadrons were designated to provide beach cover, while another fifteen squadrons protected the fleet. An additional thirty-three fighter squadrons were tasked for escort duties with the bombers and airborne forces. Thirty-six bomber squadrons were to provide direct support to the land battle with seven additional squadrons of Spitfires and Mustangs providing fire control.

In total some 5,000 fighters were operating over the invasion area in addition to the medium and heavy bombers. Between 6 and 30 June this Allied air fleet would conduct a total of 163,403 air sorties.

Using this vast air capability at the Allies disposal, Tedder directed Bomber Command to attack targets throughout France by night while the U.S. Eighth Air Force along with fleets of Allied fighter bombers attacked other selected targets by day.

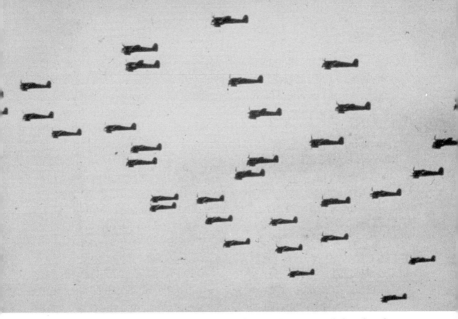

Typhoons en-masse, by D-Day the Allies had won total domination of the skies.

The outcome of this air campaign was dramatic. From January 1944 to D-Day the French rail system was strangled as a result of the thorough execution of the *Transportation Plan.* German controlled French rail traffic dropped to a mere thirty percent of its 1943 totals. Essential bridges leading to the Normandy battle area were destroyed and all major roads and railways severely damaged. From 1 April to 5 June, the allied air force made 200,00 offensive and defensive sorties. Montgomery described this effort as 'brilliant.' To support the BODYGUARD deception plans for D-Day these attacks were not confined to Normandy alone. Raids were conducted across northern France and Belgium. The Seine and Loire River bridges were particularly singled out for methodical destruction in May 1944, thereby impeding the movement of the critical panzer and panzergrenadier divisions into Normandy after D-Day. Innovation was the spirit of this time. Allied air force commanders initiated new tactics such as shuttle bombing, improved radar equipment, and developed fuel drop tanks in order to extend aircraft ranges. This was a magnificent effort. As J. Flagg stated in his work on the United States Army Air Force in World War II, 'the Anglo-American Air Forces did more than facilitate the historical invasion of 6 June 1944, they made it possible.'

Because of the very thorough and integrated Allied planning involved in every aspect of Operation OVERLORD the Germans were unable to assess this bombing campaign and deduce with any certainty as to where the expected invasion would take place. This confusion was reinforced by the Allied air targeting policy: for every raid inside Normandy two were conducted elsewhere. The effects of the bombing operations were severe and felt throughout the West. In 1946 Lieutenant General Friedrich Dihm, former Special Assistant to Erwin Rommel, stated in an interrogation conducted by the US Army:

'Except for this air supremacy, it would have been possible, in my opinion, to prevent a successful invasion during the first days after the initial assault. These were the most critical days for the Allies. Later, the constant and increasing reinforcement of the Allies could be less and less equalized by the arrival of German reinforcements, hindered by the destruction of important traffic routes.'

The air plan combined the strengths of both the bomber force and tactical air assets with devastating results. Part of Tedder's overall strategy was to draw out the enemy air force and destroy it in combat. The effects of this policy were dramatic. By June 1944 the Allies dominated the skies above the Neptune-Overlord area. From January to June 1944 a total of 2,262 German fighter pilots had been killed out of a force averaging 2,283 at any one time. In May 1944 alone, twenty-five percent of the total fighter pilot force had died during a relentless Anglo-American campaign to rid the skies over France of enemy aircraft. From April 1944 waves of air attacks were mounted against enemy airfields within a 130-mile radius of the invasion beaches.

It is hardly surprising that the Luftwaffe would be notably ineffective on D-Day. Only two German fighters would strafe the beaches during the daytime.

Beyond the lodgment area Allied air power would be a major contributor to the disruption and delay of German troop and equipment movements. At the St Paul's briefing Montgomery had stated: 'Air must hold the ring...and make very difficult the movement of enemy reserves by train or road towards the lodgment area.' After 6 June one mobile *Kampfgruppen* ordered to move from Brittany to Normandy took ten days to reach the invasion front as a result of sustained Allied air attacks.

Unfortunately, at the tactical level, even the might of the Allied air forces would fall short of expectations at Sword and Omaha Beaches on D-Day. At 0600 hours some 480 B-24 Liberator bombers of the US 8th Air Force were to attack thirteen targets along the coast. In limited visibility many of those raids were initiated late or abandoned for fear of bombing the convoys or landing craft already heading in to the shore. As a result, the bombs fell harmlessly inland leaving the defenses intact and the flat open beaches un-cratered and thus devoid of cover for the approaching waves of assault troops. In Colleville near Ouistreham, strongpoint Hillman, which was one of the strongest depth fortifications in Normandy and sited directly inland from Sword Beach, was left unscathed. The planned air raid had been aborted because of low cloud cover over the target.

The Joint Campaign: Naval Forces

While Allied air forces could shape the battlefield, provide force protection and isolate the invasion area it would inevitably fall to the combined fleet of the Allied navies to get the expeditionary armies to their objectives. Allied naval forces were under the overall command of Admiral Sir Bertram Ramsay. His tasks included the design and preparation of Operation NEPTUNE the maritime element of the OVERLORD invasion plan. Some 4,100 ships and craft of all types would be involved in the initial assault, each vessel choreographed into the grand design, the object of which – as Ramsay stated in his orders — was to 'secure a lodgment on the continent from which further offensive operations can be developed.'

Ramsay's responsibilities included the carriage and sustainment of the invasion forces in Normandy. In addition naval gunfire would form a vital, devastating component in the overall fire support provided to the ground forces during their assault and into the follow-on phase when the lodgment would be secured. Naval gunfire would also prove to be a decisive component in offensive and defensive fire missions during the Battle of Normandy. This intimate tactical support would continue while the front line remained within range of the ship guns sited off the beaches. Naval assets would also play a major role in the FORTITUDE deception operations by supporting a feint towards the Pas de Calais.

The Eastern Naval Task Group was responsible for Gold, Juno, and Sword Beaches.

Admiral Sir Bertram Home Ramsay

The British Commonwealth assault area extended from the eastern boundary of Omaha Beach just west of Port-en-Bessin to the river Orne at Ouistreham, a distance of some twenty-five miles. The Eastern Task Group had to contend with the threat of coastal shore batteries, the heavy guns of Le Havre and the threat of *Schnellboots* or 'S' Boats from the flotilla stationed in Le Havre.

The Task Group was under the overall command of Rear Admiral Sir Philip Vian RN. Lieutenant General Sir Miles C. Dempsey would accompany him on his flagship HMS *Scylla*, a Dido-class cruiser. Vian was responsible for supporting Dempsey's 2nd Army with over 200 vessels of all types. His command was divided into subordinate Forces: Force 'G' under Commodore Cyril E. Douglas-Pennant RN would support 50th (Northumbrian) Division at Gold Beach. Force 'J' under Commodore Geoffrey N. Oliver RN would land and then support 3rd Canadian Division ashore at Juno Beach. Force 'S' under Rear Admiral Arthur G. Talbot RN would support 3rd British Division ashore. A Follow-up Force 'L' under Rear Admiral William E. Parry RN would be responsible for landing various follow-on elements on all three beaches.

An additional protective task involved the defense of the invasion fleet from enemy naval action. On D-Day the Allied naval commanders were acutely aware of the threat posed by German 'S' (motor torpedo boats or E-Boats as they were known by the Allies) stationed in the fortified ports of Le Havre and Cherbourg.

Just over five weeks earlier, on 28 April 1944, the American convoy T4 had been attacked by E-Boats in Lyme Bay off the Dorset coast while taking part in Exercise TIGER. This exercise was an invasion dress rehearsal for the US VIIth Corps. The convoy was carrying men from the 4th Infantry Division destined for the operation against Utah Beach on D-Day. The three-mile long convoy consisted of eight LCTs under the escort of HMS *Azalea*. Shortly after 0200 hours the convoy was attacked by nine E-Boats from the 5th and 9th Flotillas in Cherbourg. The results were devastating. Three LCTs were struck in less than twenty-five minutes. US personnel commented afterwards that the Germans had them 'trapped and hemmed-in like a bunch of wolves circling a wounded dog.' A total of 749 men were killed. One unit, the 3206th Quartermaster Company was annihilated.

At dawn the following day rescue ships approached the area. Aboard HMS *Obedient* Julien Perkin recalled:

'We arrived in the area at daybreak and the sight was appalling.
There were hundreds of bodies of American servicemen in full battle

gear, floating in the sea. Many had their limbs and even their heads blown off... Of all those we took on board there were only nine survivors.'

Fortunately on D-Day the combined fleet would prove highly effective in deterring further German forays from the ports on the flanks of the invasion area. Sword, the eastern most assault area, provided the only example of German surface operations against the NEPTUNE fleet. Once confusing reports in the early hours of 6 June had alerted Admiral Krancke's naval command that something was afoot, he ordered units from his Western Defense Force to conduct patrols. At 0430 hours three torpedo boats (T-28, *Jaguar* and *Mowe*) from 5. *Torpedobootsflotille* sailed from Le Havre to sweep the Baie de la Seine under command of *Korvettenkapitan* Heinrich Hoffmann. At approximately 0530 hours they exited from an air delivered smoke screen and found themselves approaching the flank of the Eastern Task Force. Eighteen torpedoes were launched. Remarkably, given the concentration of targets, only one ship would be lost in this German naval action on D-Day and that was the Royal Norwegian Navy's destroyer, the *Svenner*, supporting Force 'S' off Ouistreham. *Svenner* was hit amidships, breaking its back and sinking with great loss. Another torpedo narrowly missed Admiral Talbot's flagship HMS *Largs* that had to take evasive action to avoid damage. Two further torpedoes passed between *Ramilles* and *Warspite*. Admiral Talbot subsequently described the British response:

'The Warspite followed the enemy in [to Le Havre] *by radar and opened fire at 14,000 yards; she reported one torpedo boat sunk.'*

Hoffmann received the Knight's Cross as an award for his exploits.

In general it is clear that the *Kriegsmarine* had ignored Admiral Donitz speech on 17 April 1944 when he demanded of his units:

'Throw yourselves recklessly into the fight...any man who

HMS Warspite in action supporting the D-Day landings.

fails to do so will be destroyed in shame and ignominy.'

The Allied navies also performed a vital fire support function bombarding German shore positions. Because of tidal variations the H-Hour for Sword Beach was 0725 hours, nearly an hour later than the landings at Omaha and Utah. The bombardment force used this time to great effect delivering additional observed and predicted fires onto coastal targets. During this essential process HMS *Warspite*, veteran of the battle of Jutland, was straddled by fire from the Seine batteries but soon changed station to avoid further harassment and then continued the delivery of devastating high-calibre shells to selected German strongpoints. This vital service to the land component would continue well into July as the land campaign remained within range of the offshore ships guns.

The Bombarding Force D mission was 'to assist in ensuring the safe and timely of our forces by the engagement of hostile coastal defenses.' Force D was dedicated to support 3rd Division and Force 'S'. Rear Admiral W. R. Patterson was the senior officer of Bombarding Force D. In total, his Force consisted of the battleships HMS *Warspite* and HMS *Ramilles*, the Monitor HMS *Roberts* and the cruisers HMS *Mauritius*, *Arethusa*, *Frobisher*, *Danae* and *Dragon* (Polish Navy). In addition a squadron of thirteen destroyers provided additional security and firepower (including the ill-fated *Svenner*). Patterson's most powerful battleship was HMS *Ramilles* with her eight 15-inch guns each capable of firing a 1,938 lbs shell over 32,000 yards (some eighteen miles). Each gun had 110 rounds aboard. Her twelve 6-inch guns provided additional firepower with 130x112 lbs shells for each gun.

While there was a particular threat to Sword sector posed by the heavy coastal batteries located astride the Seine estuary, additional batteries further west at Villerville, Mount Canisy and Houlgate were also identified and designated as priority targets for each of the two battleships and the monitor in Force D. The bombardment and suppression of these shore batteries commenced at 0545 hours. The attacks on the closer range batteries and coastal defenses would also be a task for the cruiser force and the destroyers. Meanwhile the Seine batteries would be engaged and then blinded by flanking smoke screens laid by Allied aircraft. In total, five naval bombardment groups were organized to engage the twenty-three German shore based batteries located in Normandy. In addition, each ship in every group was given one battery as its primary target. Reconnaissance and intelligence gathering operations prior to D-Day had identified and mapped these battery positions in great detail.

Types of German batteries that would oppose the landings: Concrete casemates housing the largest calibre pieces and more vulnerable open emplacements.

Initially Force D's main effort was focussed on German coastal gun batteries, fortifications on the beaches, and on-call interdiction missions against possible reserves deploying to the lodgment area. But once the land component commenced the assault at 0725 hours, the navy would provide on-call fire support. The destroyer force would then move to the flanks of each assault sector and continue bombarding identified targets.

To provide accurate targeting the NEPTUNE bombardment forces were supported by 104 spotter planes and thirty-nine Forward Observer Bombardment (FOB) parties. The FOB parties consisted of naval personnel equipped with radio communications back to the ships and trained to operate with the ground forces ashore. The air spotters were equipped with slow moving Piper aircraft, ideal for loitering and observing over the battlefield. The air spotters made a vital contribution to the effectiveness of naval gunfire support during the landing phase. As a result of their target indication and adjustment of fire, targets were actually engaged up to seventeen miles inland. This was endorsed in the privately published history of the 21st Panzer Division that stated,

'The enemy dominated important road junctions and supply routes with recce aircraft. He bombed or fired at central points, sometimes also with heavy naval guns at long range.'

The preliminary bombardment at Sword Beach would prove sufficient to disrupt or damage many of the inland defenses threatening 3rd Division's advance. However, where beach defenses had been sited to fire along the beach in enfilade (fire applied to a target from the flank rather than head on) such as strongpoint Cod, many bunkers and gun emplacements were hard to see from offshore and these remained unscathed and combat effective. Indeed, once the initial bombardment had finished, many of the German defenders from the 736th Coastal Defense Regiment were able to pull themselves together and man their positions against the incoming landing craft.

During his subsequent and increasingly desperate attempts to contain and eliminate the bridgehead, Rommel reported,

'Our operations in Normandy are tremendously hampered ...by...the superiority of the enemy air force [and] the effect of the heavy naval guns.'

After the war other German generals would also praise the naval gunfire support provided in Normandy. Field Marshal von Rundstedt said, 'The fire from your battleships was a main factor in hampering our counter-attacks. This was a big surprise...'

The British Ground Force Component

Second British Army

Under command of Lieutenant General Miles 'Bimbo' Dempsey the Second (2nd) British Army issued its final Operation Order No.1 on 21st April 1944. The Army would be landing with 30th Corps right (West) and 1st Corps left (East) with three divisions up and five assault brigades in the first echelon. The inter-Corps boundary was exclusive to 1st Corps: La Riviere, Tierceville, Fresnay le Crotteur, and inclusive Putot en Bessin. The stated Second Army intention was to:

(a) Assault between PORT EN BESSIN 7587 and the R ORNE.

(b) Secure and develop a bridgehead South of the line CAUMONT 7059-CAEN 0368-and SE of CAEN in order to secure airfield sites and to protect the flank of First US Army while the latter captures CHERBOURG and the BRITTANY Ports.'

The Army concept of operations was broken down in to four detailed phases. This extract only covers 1st Corps of which, 3rd Division was a critical component and the specific subject of this study:

'Phase I

On D Day 1 Corps will:

1. Assault the beaches between 940865 (incl) – R ORNE (incl).

2. Capture CAEN.

3. Secure a firm base on the general line PUTOT EN BESSIN 9072 (incl)-CAEN (incl).

4. Seize the coastal defences FRANCEVILLE 1578-CABOURG 2179 from the rear and dominate OUISTREHAM 1079-CABOURG 2179-TROARN 1667-CAEN in order to secure the left flank and prevent interference with the beaches immediately West of OUISTREHAM.

5. Operate in front of the firm base with an armoured force with the objective of securing EVRECY 9259.'

Additional tasks included the capture and guarding of Wasserman, Wurtzburg, and Freya radars within boundaries.

In Phase II the Corps was tasked to pivot on Caen and maintain contact with 30th Corps on its right. This would then lead into Phase III when the Corps would secure high ground between Caen and Falaise around Bretteville sur Laize and Argence in order to allow airfields to be built southeast of Caen. Unfortunately this area would not be taken until August 1944 and then not without enormous cost to the Commonwealth and Polish forces engaged there (Operation TOTALISE). In Phase IV the Corps was to gain contact with First US Army at VIRE.

**Lieutenant General
Sir John Crocker.**

1st British Corps

Lieutenant General Sir John Crocker commanded 1st British Corps. Crocker was an experienced veteran from World War I when he had won a DSO, MC, and Croix de Guerre. He had a sharp incisive mind, an honest character and a tendency to be a strict disciplinarian. In 1944 his Corps consisted of three infantry divisions (3rd British, 3rd Canadian, and 51st Highland) two of which were reinforced with supporting armoured brigades. An additional armoured brigade (33rd) was retained under Corps command. The 80th Anti-Aircraft Brigade and the normal component of support assets were also in place to support the Corps.

The 1st Corps *Operation Order No. 1* was issued on 5th May 1944. Dealing only with operations ashore it stated the intention and tasks for the Army, flanking formations and the specific divisions under General Crocker's command. It stated:

The Assault

1 Corps will assault, 3rd Canadian Infantry Division RIGHT, two brigades up; 3rd British Infantry Division LEFT, one brigade up.

It will be the task of these divisions to secure the covering position on the general line PUTOT EN BESSIN 9072 – CAEN – thence River ORNE to the sea on D-Day.

The tasks of the assaulting divisions is to break through the coastal defences and advance some ten miles inland on D day.

Great speed and boldness will be required to achieve this. It will be necessary to forestall the action of the enemy's local reserves quickly, overcome minor resistance met during the advance, to get set before the arrival of reserve formations, and be ready to meet the enemy's first counter attacks, which must be expected to develop by the evening of D-Day.

As soon as the beach defences have been penetrated therefore, not a moment must be lost in beginning the advance inland. Armour should

50

be used boldly from the start. Such an action will forestall the enemy's reaction, confuse him, magnify his fears and enable ground to be made quickly.

All available artillery must be ready to support the advance. If opposition is met which cannot be overcome by these strong advance guards, simple plans embodying the full resources of artillery and armour must be employed to dislodge the enemy quickly and certainly. Hastily staged, ill-supported infantry attacks are unlikely to succeed and are likely to be slow and costly in the long run.'

What is crucial to note here is the emphasis on speed and momentum.

The 3rd British Division: Order of Battle

The War Establishment was set at about 17,000 men but this excluded those special attachments that would join the division specifically for the assault phase of the invasion. Of those 17,000 men, less than half were actually infantrymen in the infantry brigades. About one quarter, or 4,500 personnel, were the officers and men of the rifle companies – the fighting edge of the division. With that in mind it is worth recording here that over the ten month period from June 1944 to the fall of Germany, the division suffered 11,084 battle casualties (the vast majority from the combat arms) and a further 6,000 non-battle casualties – all men lost from the division. The reality was that very few of those men in the rifle companies taking part in Operation Overlord on that cold grim morning on 6 June 1944 were likely to see the Normandy campaign through to the end unscathed.

Two of the three subordinate formations of the division were 8 and 9 Infantry Brigades. These brigades had fought together under the then Major General Bernard Montgomery's command in France in May-June 1940 and successfully withdrawn, in comparatively good order, from France through Dunkirk under his strong leadership. In 1942 the 185 Infantry Brigade joined the division.

Each of the three infantry brigades

3rd Division badge.

consisted of three infantry battalions. Each of those nine infantry battalions in the division consisted of a support company with four platoons: mortar platoon with six 3-inch mortars, a carrier platoon with thirteen Bren Carriers and an anti-tank platoon equipped with six of the ubiquitous 6-Pounder guns, and the assault pioneer platoon. The four rifle companies each had three platoons, each of three ten-man sections, with one light machinegun in each section. The rifle companies also held three Projector Infantry Anti-Tanks or PIATs. These were inferior man-portable, spring loaded, and short-range antitank projectors with a maximum effective range of about 50 yards. Total battalion manpower strength would number 821 all ranks.

An additional infantry battalion, the 2nd Middlesex Regiment, also featured in the divisional Order of Battle for OVERLORD and subsequent operations up to the end of the War. The Middlesex Regiment was a key component in the division's combat organization, providing each of the three brigades with 'Support Groups'. Each Support Group consisted of twelve Vickers medium machine guns and four 4.2-inch mortars; a substantial addition to the combat power available to brigade commanders.

The division also had an armoured reconnaissance regiment (Royal Armoured Corps) that was one of only two Territorial Army units in the division. The armoured reconnaissance regiment had been formed from the 8th Battalion, The Royal Northumberland Fusiliers. It consisted of a Headquarters (HQ) Squadron and three Reconnaissance (recce) Squadrons. The HQ Squadron had an anti-tank battery of eight 6-pounders, a mortar troop with six 3-inch mortars and signal and administration troops.

The recce squadrons each consisted of one HQ and three recce troops equipped with Humber armoured cars, Bren Carriers and an assault troop of infantry mounted in half-tracks. The total armoured fighting vehicle strength in this regiment was twenty-eight half tracks, twenty-four light recce Humbers, and sixty-three Bren Carriers with a total manpower strength of 41 officers and 755 other ranks.

The division's artillery was divided up and 'tied' to each infantry brigade. The 76th Highland Field Regiment (TA) was in support of 8 Brigade. 33rd Field Regiment was in support of 9 Brigade, while 7th Field was supporting 185 Brigade. Field regiments had a total of 24 guns and carried 144 rounds of high explosive at 'first line' (immediately available within the forward battle area), in addition to sixteen smoke and twelve armoured piercing (AP) rounds per gun.

A battery from each field regiment supported its own designated battalion of infantry. Each battery was equipped with eight American manufactured self-propelled M7 'Priests' carrying the 105-mm howitzer mounted on an adapted Sherman tank chassis. The priest was capable of providing fire support to the assault forces as they moved onto the beach by shooting from the open decks of their LCTs and

LCAs. By D-Day this had become a well-practiced drill developed during the 'live' firing rehearsals conducted in Scotland at the Divisional Battle School, during the training and build up phase prior to D-Day.

This technique allowed the guns to fire over the bows on the run-in from 11,000 yards down to 4,000 yards, at which point they prepared for beaching. During the 'run-in shoot' as it was called, they would fire off about 100 rounds per gun. The ammunition would be stacked on the open decks around the Priests. Unfortunately, the Priests were soon withdrawn from British service and replaced by towed 25-pounders because the Americans could not provide sufficient 105 mm ammunition to their own artillery units in addition to British artillery units. Similarly the four batteries of 20th Anti-tank Regiment (RA) were 'brigaded' in the same way as the field regiments. To a lesser extent so were the batteries of the 92nd Light Anti-Aircraft Regiment (RA). This regiment had been formed from the 7th Battalion The Loyal Regiment. The 92nd Light Anti-Aircraft Regiment was organised into three batteries each of three troops, each of six 40-mm guns giving a total of fifty-four air defence guns.

The 20th Anti-tank Regiment had a total of forty-eight guns and was equipped with one troop of American self-propelled M10s that carried a 3-inch gun on a Sherman chassis. This was a fine anti-tank weapon with only slightly less penetrating power than the 17-pounder. The other two troops in each battery were using towed 17-pounders that would require greater handling over the sands of Sword Beach.

3rd Division Units

The division's engineers consisted of three field companies and a field park company under command of HQ Royal Engineers (HQRE). 246 Field Company was under command of 8 Infantry Brigade. The Company's task was to carry out assault demolitions, hand mine clearance tasks and the opening of one wheeled route forward to the Brigade objective at Periers-sur-le-Dan. Field Park Companies contained a workshop and a stores platoon, their tasks being to act as a base for the field companies and hold specialist and bulky equipment including bulldozers. Field companies had 257 all ranks. The divisional bridging troop held 80-feet of Bailey bridging capable of carrying 40-ton loads. 253 Field Company, less one platoon, were to open and maintain safe lanes consisting of one single and one double-way route for 185 Infantry Brigade close behind the advance. The other platoon under command of 9 Infantry brigade was to provide assault demolition and mine clearance teams.

7 Field Company, with 71 Field Company and detachments of 106 Bridging Company Royal Army Service Corps were attached from Army and GHQ Engineers. Their task was to clear a wheeled route to Benouville and then construct and operate Class 5 ferry and Class 40 bridges over the Caen canal and river Orne at Benouville and Ranville. 15 Field Park Company was to provide bulldozer teams for the field companies, take over local stores dumps, and establish Engineer RVs to reload returned empty bridging company vehicles.

For the assault task, the division took under command the 27 Armoured Brigade with 190 Shermans and 33 Stuart light tanks. One unit, the 13/18th Hussars would deploy from their LCTs 5,000 yards offshore and strike out for the beach in their unseaworthy Duplex Drive (DD) 'amphibious' Sherman tanks. The two other armoured regiments of 27 Armoured Brigade were the Staffordshire Yeomanry and the East Ridings Yeomanry both equipped with Shermans and Stuarts. The brigade numbered 3,400 all ranks and 1,200 vehicles; a sizable addition to the division.

There were of course additional attachments for D-Day. The 4th Royal Marine (RM) Commando and the bulk of 1st Special Service (unfortunately abbreviated to SS) Brigade was placed under command until the landing was made. Once ashore they were to pass through the leading brigade positions and move on to join up with 6th Airborne Division at Benouville and beyond the east bank of the river Orne. In addition, the 53rd Medium Regiment (RA), 5th Independent RM Armoured Support Battery and two detachments of RM frogmen, who were to clear beach obstacles, were also under command. A slice of the 5th Assault Regiment RE and detachments of the 22nd and the Westminster Dragoons equipped with flail tanks and an assortment of 'funnies' from Hobart's 79th Armoured Division were also provided. Additional engineer resources from the Army Group were to assist the assault groups to clear four zones of beach obstacles, clear routes and glider landing sites for the follow up waves of 6th Airborne Division, and to bridge the river Orne and its canal.

The great majority of these attachments were present to help the assault division over the first physical and psychological obstacle of the open beach and through the initial crust of German defences. The major exception would be the 101st Beach Sub Area which would be responsible for the landing of all men, vehicles and stores for the division (along with those belonging to 6th Airborne Division and a slice of supplies for the 1st Corps troops) right up to D + 55.

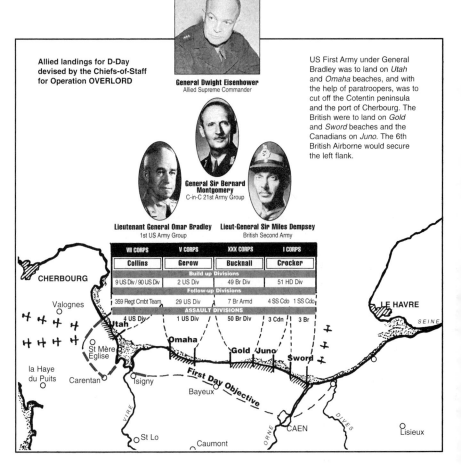

Allied landings for D-Day devised by the Chiefs-of-Staff for Operation OVERLORD

General Dwight Eisenhower
Allied Supreme Commander

US First Army under General Bradley was to land on *Utah* and *Omaha* beaches, and with the help of paratroopers, was to cut off the Cotentin peninsula and the port of Cherbourg. The British were to land on *Gold* and *Sword* beaches and the Canadians on *Juno*. The 6th British Airborne would secure the left flank.

General Sir Bernard Montgomery
C-in-C 21st Army Group

Lieutenant General Omar Bradley
1st US Army Group

Lieut-General Sir Miles Dempsey
British Second Army

VII CORPS	V CORPS	XXX CORPS	I CORPS
Collins	Gerow	Bucknall	Crocker
Build up Divisions			
9 US Div / 90 US Div	2 US Div	49 Br Div	51 HD Div
Follow-up Divisions			
359 Regt Cmbt Team	29 US Div	7 Br Armd	4 SS Cdo 1 SS Cdo
ASSAULT DIVISIONS			
4 US Div	1 US Div	50 Br Div	3 Cdn 3 Br

CHERBOURG

Valognes

Utah

Omaha

Gold Juno

Sword

LE HAVRE

SEINE

St Mère Eglise

la Haye du Puits

Carentan

Isigny

First Day Objective

Bayeux

VIRE

St Lo

Caumont

ORNE

CAEN

DIVES

Lisieux

A Joint and Combined Force

It is important to note that the 3rd Infantry Division, its brigades, or even its proud regiments, cannot be thought of in isolation. The success of the division depended on a close co-operation between all Arms and Services that comprised the total force. Battalions and brigades all relied on the support provided by the Royal Artillery (RA), the Royal Engineers (RE), the Royal Signals (RSignals), the Royal Army Service Corps (RASC), the Royal Army Medical Corps (RAMC), the Royal Electrical & Mechanical Engineers (REME) and the Corps of Military Police (CMP).

NEPTUNE-OVERLORD was to be the greatest amphibious operation of the war. The division was carried and supported by Naval Force 'S' or Sword, commanded by Rear Admiral A. G. Talbot. His flagship for Neptune would be HMS *Largs*, a former French passenger liner, the *Charles Plumier*. Under command he also had Bombardment Force 'D' and three assault groups and associated 'Build-Up Squadrons.' HMS *Largs* would be the nerve centre from which the NEPTUNE plan for Sword Beach would be controlled and directed. Once the General Officer Commanding 3rd Division established himself ashore, command of land operations would be switched from the sea-based headquarters to Rennie's forward command post, initially in Hermanville.

As early as December 1943, the 3rd Division had started to concentrate around Inverness and the Moray Firth for a series of amphibious exercises with the maritime component of Force Sword under Talbot. A unique and intimate sense of team spirit rapidly developed between the naval force and its designated division. To his credit Talbot established his HQ alongside Divisional HQ in Cameron Barracks, Inverness. He also saw to it that every assault vessel under his command bore the 3rd Division's glorious and unmistakable triangular badge.

Through December 1943 Talbot's small armada of landing craft and ships were harboured from Invergordan to Fort George on the south side of the Moray Firth. From here a series of grueling exercises were conducted in harsh sea states through the winter and early spring. After the invasion Rear Admiral Talbot would report that the hard school in which the Force had trained in the Moray Firth was a blessing in disguise. Soldiers and sailors of Force 'S' had been well prepared for the rigors of expeditionary operations by the time D-Day was upon them.

Above the invasion fleet would be the 5,000 fighters and the medium and heavy bomber armadas of the British and American tactical air forces. With proper coordination, leadership, courage and thorough planning this joint and combined force would be able to punch a hole through the Atlantic Wall and liberate France, occupied Western Europe and then ultimately defeat Nazi Germany.

But let us not forget that for all this apparent invincibility, the close-contact battle on the beaches and inland could still be lost against the German Army. This was not a foe that could be brushed aside or in any way underestimated. Events at Omaha Beach certainly demonstrated this, as did the brilliantly executed actions conducted at the tactical level by Waffen-SS and panzer grenadier units, frequently with little sound strategic or operational direction, adequate air support, or any real hope of decisive victory.

CHAPTER THREE

THE OVERLORD ASSAULT PLAN: SWORD BEACH AND CAEN

OVERLORD planners had sought information from all available sources on such matters as water depths, beach contours, gradients, tidal patterns, and coastal obstructions such as reefs, soft sand patches, or sandbars. Beyond the beaches the terrain was further assessed for its suitability as a defensible lodgment, as a logistic base for subsequent operations, for the siting of improvised air landing grounds, and for avenues of approach inland for the breakout.

This detailed analysis drew on all sources of information including pre-war holiday postcards and family snapshots gathered from a willing public throughout Britain. Special Forces personnel, in addition to air, navy and army intelligence assets also conducted active military reconnaissance operations. The secret army of local French Resistance operatives also provided timely information. On display in the Museum of Peace in Caen, are examples of their intricate hand-drawn sketches and maps made by these French patriots in Normandy throughout 1943-44. The precision and detail of such intricate work is breathtaking.

From bases in England, electronic surveillance systems also monitored all the intercepted radio emissions from occupied Europe. Radar sites command headquarters and unit locations were detected, identified and integrated into the vast intelligence mosaic that would ultimately shape the Allies plans for the great counter-invasion in the West. The most notable source of signal intelligence came from the Ultra intercepts. As Group Captain Desmond Young a veteran of 123 Wing in 2nd ATF wrote in his memoir *Typhoon Pilot*, 'The preparations were staggering...The scale and precision of it all made our past efforts look insignificant.'

The coast in 1st Corps sector consisted of flat sandy beaches with rocky outcrops above the low water mark along the whole sector except for two short stretches at the mouth of the Rivers Seulles and Orne. It was also assessed that there were clay patches that would hamper beach movement for vehicles in the western half of the sector. The beaches were generally backed-up by sand dunes. Sea walls or even low cliffs provided additional obstacles to vehicle movement. Inland of the dunes, the ground to this day rises to about 200 feet in a rolling expanse of cultivated farmland.

On the right (western flank) of the 1st Corps area, the River Seulles and its tributaries (including the Thue and Chiromme) formed obstacles to movement by wheeled if not tracked vehicles. On the left (eastern flank), the Caen Canal and river Orne formed major north-south obstacles to all lateral movement. The water level in the former was controlled by lock gates in Ouistreham and by a barrage in Caen. The lock gates were defended by bunker positions with armoured cupolas. Beyond the Orne to the East, thickly wooded, dominant high ground divides the valley of the River Orne from the valley of the river Dives.

In 1944 the Germans frequently made a five to fifteen mile zone,

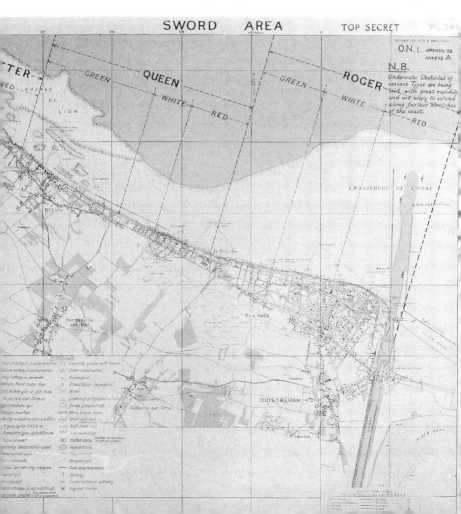

from the seashore inland, off-limits though fishermen and farmers were usually allowed to maintain their trades. Within Sword sector the town of Ouistreham dominated the coastline. Going west along the assault beach, the smaller holiday settlements at Hermanville and Lion sur Mer provided navigational reference points to the boat crews and fortifiable strongpoints to the German defenders. Behind this narrow coastal crust of settlements, the ground rises gently towards Cresserons, Periers Ridge and Colleville. That dominant curve of higher ground offers superb views of the Channel, the coastline and the far bank of the Orne. Not surprisingly, German strongpoints around Colleville were sited there on dominant features. Behind the Periers Ridge and to the south towards Caen, the ground becomes more complex with a series of valleys and ridges interspersed with villages connected by narrow roads. Just north of Caen the ground rises to what was formerly the thickly wooded Lebisey Ridge. The ridge then falls away into the city of Caen.

With a few exceptions the OVERLORD lodgment area was not suitable for heavy military traffic. So the unfortunate assault troops would be committed to moving inland into the traditional Norman countryside known as bocage. Bocage denotes high hedges grown on earthen embankments to separate fields, crops and ownership. These high earthworks and the overhanging tree canopy and foliage often overshadowed roads and tracks. In 1944 the bocage would be a godsend to the defender and a nightmare to the attacker. Today, few examples remain in the British sector as fields have been expanded and roads widened. Good examples of bocage can still be seen in the Suisse Normande around Falaise and behind Omaha and Utah Beaches.

German Defences in Normandy

In May 1944 a signal from the Japanese naval attaché in Berlin to Tokyo was intercepted by British intelligence and decoded. It confirmed that Rommel intended to destroy any invasion 'near the coast, most of all on the beaches.' To that end Rommel had designed an overall defensive scheme for the Normandy sector consisting of three belts. The first belt was sited on or immediately behind the beaches and consisted of a narrow band of obstacles covered by fire from coastal defense units. A second line consisting of strongpoints up to five miles inland was under construction. By June 1944 this second line was still incomplete. At Sword Beach, however, strongpoint Hillman (located inland from La Breche D'Hermanville) dominated the back-beach area and was very much complete.

Beach defences along the invasion coast were being improved daily.

So while a rigorous battle could be fought at the water's edge and in the backbeach zone, should any penetration be made beyond this fortified area, the thin belt of initially strong positions along the coast and in the deep draws would became inherently vulnerable to being rolled-up from the flank. This threat could only be countered by local mobile reserves able to mount immediate and effective counter attacks. Should these initial lines of resistance be penetrated then Rommel would have to call upon his third line of defense, the operational reserves, which could initially fix and then destroy any Allied breakthrough.

To reinforce the foreshore defences, the Germans were seen to be building new obstacles along the Norman coast by February 1944, under the direction of Rommel. The 3rd British Infantry Division's 'Briefing Intelligence Summary' described the defences they would be facing at Sword Beach, however the general assessment was applicable to all the beaches. It stated:

'Defence activity has quickened since February on the occupied coasts, following a tour of inspection in January by ROMMEL, who is anti-invasion Army Group Commander. The principal new features are under-water obstacles, the provision of overhead cover for field and medium artillery, an intensification of minelaying, and a tendency to dig field defences on commanding ground 2,000-4,000 yards inland.'

The Beach obstacles were sited in three bands and designed to impede or defeat landing operations between the high and low water marks across the tidal flat. The outer obstacle strip consisted of reinforced iron structures known as 'Element C.' These gate-like structures stood ten feet high and had Teller anti-tank mines lashed to their upright supports. The Element C obstacles were sited about 250 meters below the high water line. The second line of obstacles were sited a further 25 metres toward the beach. This belt consisted of mine, or shell, tipped wooden posts, each one foot thick, driven into the sand at a shallow angle and supported by an 'A' frame. These ramp type obstacles were usually sited in two rows between thirty to sixty feet apart with about fifty feet between individual obstacles. The angle was such that these obstacles would present a major threat to the hull of any approaching vessel as the tide covered the line of eught to ten foot high posts between one and two hours before high tide. On D-Day this particular line of obstacles would prove to be a formidable barrier to landing craft.

Tellermines were attached to the tops of wooden stakes.

The final lines of submerged barriers were sited one hundred and

Three girders bolted together at the centre, and set in concrete blocks, were intended to cause landing craft to be concentrated into zones that were covered by the defenders' guns.

thirty yards from the shore. These consisted of steel 'hedgehogs' constructed from three or more angled steel girders crossed at their centres. Each hedgehog stood approximately five foot high and was sited in rows about 100-110 meters long, each row containing fourteen to seventeen hedgehogs at twenty foot intervals. Rows were overlapped and ran continuously across the beachfront and were submerged about an hour before high water. Intelligence assessments stated that these obstacles could sink in the sand. These hedgehogs were sufficiently strong that they could penetrate the hulls of landing craft. It is important to realize that these belts of obstacles were not continuous but were staggered to hamper the direct approach of craft to the beach. On 6 May General Eisenhower described these beach obstacles as 'one of the worst problems of these days.' Two days later, a full assessment had been made of up to date photo-reconnaissance pictures. These high-resolution pictures had allowed the positions of each obstacle to be plotted in detail. As a result of this intelligence, the Allies confirmed that the landings would commence at half-flood on the day that this came at forty minutes after nautical twilight (June 5 was ideal with possible postponements acceptable to the 6 or 7 June).

At Sword Beach the Germans had not placed loose mines on the tidal flats but sited them above and beyond the beach and around the

Mines were being laid in ever increasing numbers leading up to D-Day.
Right: Tellermine 43 and below right Tellermine 35.

German 'S' (shrapnel) anti-personnel mine. Right: fitted with pull igniters and trip wires. Dismantled S mine showing the 3-prong push igniter which operates when a light downwards pressure is applied to one of the prongs. This causes the mine to jump three feet in the air, after which a second explosion hurls the steel balls up to fifty yards.

beachfront villas. A barbed wire triple concertina obstacle belt had also been integrated into the landward defences immediately above the sands. In addition, the Germans had made full use of all available weapons including captured French and British mines from 1940. They also built a number of marked and fenced dummy minefields with pieces of metal plate buried to deceive mine detectors and so prolong and delay any clearance of the area by combat engineers.

These various simple but ingenious obstacles were covered by the fire of weapons sited in defensive positions manned by the coastal defense troops along the top of the sea wall. Many of these fire positions were sited in defilade and so protected from the direct fire from ships out to sea. The crescent shape of Sword Beach also provided the Germans with every advantage to pour flanking fire into the sides of any attacking force.

Beyond the immediate beach area there were a series of fortified strong points or resistance nests (*Widerstandsnest* or WN) that acted as 'surfaces' against which assaults would be battered. These strongpoints were sited to cover the beach exits. On 6 June several concrete emplacements were still incomplete in Sword sector, most notably at a strongpoint in Colleville, codenamed 'Morris' by the Allies. However, even the partially completed positions were still inherently capable of protecting their resident fighting crews who could then inflict heavy casualties and delays on the 1st Corps troops caught crossing the beach or the open fields beyond. A completed resistance nest normally consisted of approximately between a platoon of thirty men and a company equipped with ten machine guns, and an artillery piece inside a reinforced bunker and a supporting 50-mm cannon.

The Germans had also sited light artillery guns to cover Sword Beach. Reinforced concrete bunkers contained 75-mm or 88-mm guns. Further smaller pillboxes held lighter artillery pieces and additional antitank guns ranging from 37-mm to 75-mm were positioned to cover likely vehicle approaches. Many of the 50-mm and 75-mm guns in use by the German forces were actually Czech or French guns seized back in 1938 and 1940. These various bunker positions were further strengthened by the integration of complete tank turrets (from captured vehicles) or cupolas from the Maginot Line (as at Ouistreham) with their armament. Automatic flame-throwers were also in place at

Concete gun emplacement with a 50mm anti-tank gun and crew on the Normandy coast shortly before the invasion.

Sword Beach although there are no reports of these grim weapons being fired. Inevitably, the infantry units garrisoning the intervening trenches along the beach were issued with a full range of infantry weapons with a high concentration of machine guns.

Indirect fire support could be provided to the forward troops by mortars located in, or to the rear of the fortified strongpoints and by rocket pits sited inland on higher ground. Mortars were usually sited in 'Tobrouks,' or open topped reinforced concrete weapons pits, many of which can still be found today amongst remaining German fortifications.

For all their localized, tactical strength the German coastal defences lacked any real depth and Rommel would be severely restricted by Hitler in his use of the operational and strategic reserves so essential to his defensive concept of operations.

German Forces in the Sword Sector

The men of the 3rd Division were to face units from the Heer, namely the 716th Coastal Defence Division. This formation was part of the LXXXIV (84th) Corps, commanded by the veteran General Erich Marcks. The 716th Division had been stationed on the Normandy coast since 16 March 1942 holding the sector between the rivers Vire and Orne. The Division was under command of Major General Wilhelm Richter whose headquarters was sited in a network of ancient quarry tunnels to the north west of Caen at Folie-Couvrechef (now contained within the grounds of the Peace Museum, Caen). He had assumed command in March 1943. From January to April 1944 his defensive frontage was adjusted or reinforced as additional units from the 77th and 243rd Divisions were integrated into the coastal defences. In May a major adjustment took place when Marcks moved the 352nd Division into the line to the West of the 716th Division's two forward regiments (the I/726th and III/726th). This move went undetected by the Allies until just before D-Day.

General Erich Marcks.

Generalmajor **Wilhelm Richter.**

On 6 June the 1st Corps would face:

716th Coastal Defense Division (6 June its total strength was 7,771 men including three battalions of Eastern volunteers each of 600 men). The division consisted of two infantry regiments (the 726th and 736th) with three battalions in each, one coastal artillery regiment with twenty-eight 100 mm T 14/19 guns and twelve rocket launchers. The division also had one battery of eleven Pak 75-mm anti-tank guns and two pioneer companies. The 716 Divisional Pioneer Battalion's two companies were deployed in Mathieu and Herouvilette. In addition, the Ost Battalion 642 was to assemble in Amfreville once 84th Corps issued the full alert codeword. This force was distributed along the coast in accordance with Rommel's doctrine:

736th Regimental HQ, commanded by *Oberst* (Colonel) Krug, was located in Strongpoint Hillman (WN 17 south of Colleville) along with the 3rd Company of 642nd Eastern Battalion. Individual companies from 736th were holding strongpoints and the interconnecting outposts within 3rd Division's area of interest. These strongpoints included those resistance nests codenamed in the Neptune-Overlord plan as Cod (WN 20), and Trout (WN 20A). Along the beach the units were deployed as follows:

10/736th at La Breche d'Hermanville in WN 20.

10th and 4/736th in Colleville-Plage, equipped with two 50-mm guns and one 75-mm gun in WN 20 (Cod).

Additional troops were drawn from 2/736th and 1/736th with Kriegsmarine and Todt Organization personnel manning intervening positions reinforced by four 20-mm mobile anti-aircraft guns covering the beach area from the 716th Flak-Zug.

Inland, several batteries of the 1716th Artillery Regiment commanded by *Leutenantoberst* Knupe were sited to cover the mouth of the river Orne and adjacent beaches. Knupe had temporarily replaced *Oberst* Andersen who had gone on sick leave in May. Knupe would be killed in mid-June east of the Orne. On 6 June his units were deployed in three battalion sectors using three artillery groups (left, right, and centre). The units were deployed from West to East as follows:

Self-propelled gun battery (*Leutenant* Scharf) in Cresserons.

Colleville Battery (B/1716th) in bunkers with four T guns.

Ouistreham Battery: with the 4/1716th battery located at the water tower with four 155 mm F guns (range 10.6 Km) and the 1/1260th in Ouistreham with six 155-mm F guns. One gun was destroyed by bombardment and the remaining guns withdrew to St Aubin-d'Arquenay.

Oberst Krug, commander of 736th Regiment, making an inspection of the defences a few weeks prior to the invasion.

Additional artillery support was available from the forward-deployed artillery units of the 21st panzer Division. The 1/155th Artillery Regiment had three 100-mm guns and four 122-mm R guns from 2/155th in the area of Periers-sur-le Dan. In additional four 88-mm guns from the 2/305th Anti Aircraft Battalion were also located along the Periers Ridge in an anti-tank screen.

This was a strong dual-purpose (indirect fire and anti-tank) artillery force. It could have inflicted even greater loss on Sword Beach and the expanding bridgehead force had it been more effectively directed by the artillery command posts located near Hillman and in the fire direction tower in Ouistreham (this still exists as a museum to the Atlantic Wall).

In his post-war interrogation General Richter, formerly the commander of the 716th Coastal Defense Division, endorsed Rommel's concept of operations but recognised that what was lacking was positional depth. He had requested a reserve division to be brought up behind his 40-50 resistance points that had been 'placed along the coastline in the shape of a string of pearls.' As the Report by Naval Commander Force G stated after the battle 'the defences gave the impression of too much concrete and not enough spirits...'

A Failure of Military Intelligence?

Only one regiment (the 726th Regiment) from 716th Limited Employment (LE) Coastal Defense Division was believed to be defending Sword sector. The 716th was assessed as being a low quality, over-extended formation with poor morale and about 50% composition of Poles and Slavs in its ranks. It was also under-strength with only 7,771 men, or 35% of the establishment strength of a standard German infantry division.

The 21st Army Group believed that this poor quality division had a frontage of fifty-three miles from the Vire estuary to the Orne-Dives area in the East. As is now known this was not the whole story. Unfortunately a major adjustment of troops had actually occurred in mid-March 1944. Rommel authorized *Generaloberst* Dollman (commander of the German Seventh Army) to move the 352nd Infantry Division from its reserve location in St Lo to the coastline. Two of its regiments joined the 716th Infantry behind Gold and Omaha Beaches. The division's third regiment moved to Bayeux as a reserve, where it would be located on D-Day.

From April onwards, Allied intelligence had identified the additional reinforcement of forward positions in several coastal sectors. On 14 May 1944 it became clear that this had occurred in the 716th Infantry's area of responsibility. Photo-reconnaissance had confirmed this particularly in the area between Isigny and the River Dives but no indication of the move forward by 352nd had been detected. Montgomery's 21st Army Group staff considered this to be,

'A most unsatisfactory state of affairs that we cannot specifically identify all elements which go to make up the sector... This much is

evident – that we will on D-Day make contact immediately with 716th 709th, 243rd, the fringe of 711th and, within a very short time, 352nd Infantry and 21st Panzer.'

As late as 4 June the Allied 21st Army Group provided what was to prove a very accurate assessment of German adjustments. But by this stage the assault divisions were already in their ships, map packs opened and briefings initiated with all craft awaiting orders to sail for France. The assessment stated:

'For some time now in other areas coastal divisions have been narrowing their sectors, while divisions the role of which has hitherto been read as lay-back have nosed forward into the gaps provided by the reduced responsibility of the coastal divisions....The evidence that the same has happened on the left in the case of 716th Division is slender indeed...yet it should not be surprising if we discovered that it has two regiments in the line and one in reserve, while on its left 352nd has one regiment up and two to play...'

In the 3rd British Infantry Division's 'Intelligence Summary', the intelligence staff placed the 352nd Division in a dispersed area covering 35-40 miles and with its closest units about fifteen miles from Caen. It was considered to be:

'Formed from remnants of a division destroyed in Russia. Personnel

MkIVs of Panzer Regiment 22, 21st Panzer Division in the countryside near Caen in the early summer of 1944.

Aerial photograph taken 22 May 1944 covering the area from Queen Red, including Queen White, to Queen Green at Lion-sur-Mer

Battery position

believed very young or 35-40. Partly mechanised.... Suitably disposed to send troops (? A regt) to strengthen POLAND [codename for Caen], *attempt to check the impact of Second Army assault by counter attacks. To stabilise the situation in preparation for the armoured counter attack.*

A further gap in the Allied intelligence picture involved the detailed dispositions of the panzer reserves. At the end of February 1944 General Rennie had believed that 10th Panzer Division was the nearest armoured threat to Sword Beach. This force could be expected to strike Sword sector within four hours of receiving orders to move. To that end Rennie placed a heavy emphasis on the probability of meeting armour on D-Day. By the time the final Divisional Intelligence Summary was issued on 16 May 1944 the 21st Panzer Division was assessed as being in a general area some ten to thirty miles south of Caen. It was assumed that units from 21st Panzer Division would be met on D-Day. On 21 May SHAEF accepted what ULTRA had actually already confirmed on the 14th: the 21st Panzer Division had moved into forward around Caen. Air reconnaissance and sighting reports of tank transporters and tank tracks in open fields had confirmed that:

'The division is now close to Caen with its tanks apparently east of the Orne. The exact area of the division and its dispositions are not known, but on any reckoning it now lies but a short run from the eastern beaches of the Neptune area.'

Montgomery, Dempsey, and Crocker were certainly clear on the implications of this threat. At his 23 May briefing to his senior commanders, Dempsey estimated that the 21st Panzer Division would be met early on D-Day with 12th SS Panzer Division entering battle by the evening of the invasion.

Preparing the 3rd Division for the Mission

At Christmas 1943 Major General T G Rennie DSO, MBE had taken over command of 3rd Division from Major General Lumsden. Rennie was an experienced commander. He had escaped from the German advance in 1940 from St Valery and had then gone on to fight the Afrika Korps in the Western Desert with 51st Highland Division.

From December 1943 through to May 1944 the 3rd Division participated in a series of seven major exercises that tested many aspects of landing this complex force on a hostile shore. BURGER 1 and BURGER 2 were conducted from the Black Isle to Burghead Bay in the Moray Firth, in order to practice the whole process of marshalling the landing troops within a beach sub-area. Exercises SMASH and GRAB were both conducted in severe weather conditions during January 1944. In February, Exercise CROWN was the last exercise during which the 3rd Division practiced a two-brigade assault. In late February Exercise ANCHOR tested the concept of assaulting Sword Beach with three brigades in echelon. Exercise LEAPYEAR followed and was the last exercise conducted by the Division in the Moray Firth before the troops and their equipment were moved south into wooded areas of Hampshire and Sussex and their final embarkation camps.

Major General T. G. Rennie, DSO, MBE.

The most significant exercise codenamed FABIUS IV then occurred on 3-4 May. The purpose of this exercise was to test the arrangements for marshalling troops and vehicles, movement to the embarkation points, and the process of embarking in the correct assault groups onto the attendant ships of Force S. The troops were then landed on beaches between Littlehampton and Bognor. After FABIUS was over the troops settled into a routine in their tented camps of final preparations, fitness training, and the inevitable equipment inspections.

A notable highlight for the troops in mid-May was the introduction of a system of 32-hour passes that enabled the men to get away from their restricted accommodation. Even this came to an end at midnight on 26 May 1944 when the camps were sealed with barbed wire and guarded by armed patrols from static units. There would be no more visits to the local pub until the veterans were once again back in Britain.

Detailed briefings now began and brigade commanders briefed their subordinate commanding officers in specially prepared briefing centres that were also individually guarded. Over the next four days a sequence of briefings were given. French Francs were issued along with a guidebook to France. Some of the more cynical troops believed that this was just another deception plan.

Between 26 and 30 May the assault force was briefed in detail using sophisticated terrain models, air photographs and diagrams. Each briefing could take up to seven hours. There was a great sense of satisfaction and confidence; everybody knew their role in this 'great enterprise.' As the briefing phase came to a close the troops were moved from their camps and established in the temporary Marshalling

Camps where men and vehicles were organised in to ship loads. Battalions of the Assault Brigade were each divided into two LSIs along with many smaller units that would land in the initial waves. Most of the 3rd Division embarked either in or around Portsmouth. 185 Brigade and the first reinforcements for 8 Brigade and the KSLI embarked at Newhaven in their LCI (L). Those not landing until the third tide embarked in London or Tilbury. So by 3 June 1944 most of the Division was aboard their ships.

The following day General Eisenhower made his decision to postpone D-Day for twenty-four hours. The waiting soldiers passed the time playing 'Housey-Housey', or doing more fitness training. On 5 June the decision to go was confirmed. D-Day would be 6 June 1944. The 'Great Crusade' was on.

3rd Division: Assault Landing Plan

The 3rd Division's Operations Order had been issued on 14 May, replacing the earlier Operational Planning Instructions and the first draft of the Operations Order. Two days later the Briefing Intelligence Summary was issued. The order stated that the Division would be landing on QUEEN WHITE and RED Beaches and then advancing to capture Caen and crossings over the River Orne within the city. This would be done using an assault brigade (8 Infantry Brigade and attached No.4 and No.41 Commandos), an Intermediate Brigade (185 Brigade), and a Reserve Brigade (9 Brigade).

The landing plan directed that four LCTs each carrying four amphibious DD Sherman tanks from the 13/18 Hussars would put their fragile loads ashore at H-5 minutes. These secret weapons would then be followed by four further LCTs that would beach and deploy specialised armour from the 79th Armoured Division. These were 'Hobart's Funnies' that included flail tanks from the 22nd Dragoons, Crocodile flamethrower tanks, AVREs equipped with Petard mortars each capable of destroying fortifications and bunkers with their main armament. This armoured force would act as the spearhead for the assault companies.

While the armour would be engaging the German defences, Royal Engineer assault groups organized into breaching or gapping teams were to clear beach obstacles for the follow-on elements from the Division and 1st Corps. Their task was to cut a series of gaps through the 'petrified forest' of obstacles and mark them for follow-on craft. They would have to work fast before the rising tide (rising 20 feet in places on D-Day) covered many of the obstacles after only 30 minutes.

Sherman and Churchill tanks loaded up and ready to make the trip across the Channel. Engineer assault vehicles including bridge layer, and flail tank.

The engineers would be supported by tanks from the 79th Armoured Division fitted with bulldozer blades landing at H+35, each tank being capable of pushing obstacles out of a boat lane or crushing them into the sand.

As an initial toehold was being established, the two leading infantry companies would beach at H+7 in eight assault landing craft. At H+20 another eight LCAs would land two more infantry companies. This force would then work together to clear the German defences covering the beach. Particular emphasis was placed on clearing strongpoint Cod – an objective for both leading assault battalions. These battalions were to then push inland up to the first lateral road running from Riva Bella to Bas Lion, codenamed Pike, and thence onto their battalion objectives at Hermanville and Colleville. 8 Brigade's objective area actually contained five strongpoints Cod, Sole, Daimler, Hillman and Morris excluding the extensive flanking fortifications in Riva Bella and Ouistreham that would be cleared by the Commandos. Brigade, and divisional objectives then extended from Periers to as far south as Caen. This meant that 1st Corps (including 3rd Canadian on the right flank) had the task of establishing a beachhead some four to ten miles deep and fourteen miles wide.

Key brigade and battalion level tasks included securing objectives on the prominent ridge of high ground to the north of Caen called Lebisey Ridge. This and other planned D-Day objectives would act as blocking positions to the inevitable German counter-attack. This extensive bridgehead would also provide 1st Corps with sufficient depth to build-up troop and logistic strength for subsequent operations and give security to the vulnerable landings of follow on units during the early stages of the invasion. Behind this shield, Crocker would deploy his divisions, and link up with the 6th Airborne Division at Benouville and beyond the Orne.

At H+25 two LCAs would land the Beach Group support teams to help establish order on what could quickly become a fairly chaotic strip of fire-drenched beach. At H+60 nine LCTs would land the 105mm self-propelled artillery guns or Priests; and thirty minutes later additional tanks would beach from ten LCTs. The tenth wave would consist of twenty-one DUKWs carrying ammunition, other combat supplies and additional towed artillery. The all-powerful Beachmasters would choreograph this complex landing schedule. They would be directing forces into and then away from the beach in order to clear the shoreline for follow-up waves of men and equipment. Using flags and radio they would attempt to control the flow of assault craft from their lowering position in to the beach as the morning's events unfolded. The planning had been thorough, the rehearsals effective. Now 3rd Division would face its first action since the debacle at Dunkirk in 1940.

A summary of brigade tasks is given below:

8 BRIGADE
Brigadier E.E. 'Copper' Cass CBE DSO MC
1 Suffolk: LtCol. R.E. Goodwin DSO
2 E Yorks: LtCol. C.F. Hutchinson
1 S Lan R: LtCol. J.E.S. Stone
8 Brigade Defence Platoon

8 Brigade with under command 13th /18th Hussars (H), 5 Assault Regiment RE and 4 and 41 Commandos were to secure the beachhead to include the high ground about Periers-sur-le-Dan and St Aubin d'Arquenay. Other specific tasks included destroying the battery positions codenamed Daimler (by the water tower at Ouistreham), Morris, and Hillman.

The Brigade Operations Order No.2 was issued on 22 May. It went into great detail about the tasks for each unit under command. The intention was clear: land and capture the Periers-sur-le-Dan feature. To this was added the specific battalion objectives. Thus the two assault battalions – the 2 East Yorks on the left and the 1 South Lancashire Regiment on the right – were to destroy the enemy holding the beach defences. The reserve battalion – 1 Suffolk – was to capture Colleville-sur-Orne and the battery (Morris) to the west, and Hillman that dominated the Periers feature on the Brigade centerline. This area would then act as a firm base for the subsequent exploitation by the Division in the critical attack on Caen.

185 BRIGADE
Brigadier K.P. Smith OBE
2 Warwicks: LtCol. H.O. Herndon
1 Norfolk: LtCol. R.H. Bellamy DSO
2 KSLI: LtCol. F.J. Maurice DSO
185 Brigade Defence Platoon

185 Brigade supported by the Staffordshire Yeomanry were to land at approximately H+1.5 hours and advance to capture Caen and a bridgehead south of the city over the River Orne. This was to be carried out with speed and boldness; the sentence was underlined for extra emphasis in the orders.

185 Brigade's operations order described how Caen would be taken in a four phase operation. Initially a mobile column of the KSLI with a troop of 41 Anti-Tank Battery equipped with Self-Propelled guns, the Staffordshire Yeomanry and two troops of the Westminster Dragoons (equipped with flail tanks to clear mines) was to secure Caen as quickly as possible. The main body were to follow to move up with the 2nd Warwickshires on the right and 1st Norfolk Regiment on the left. The expected timing was that the whole brigade, including artillery and tanks would be complete by H+4 hours with Bren Carriers and towed anti-tank guns arriving an hour later: a simple and well-understood plan. Sadly it would not survive first contact with the enemy.

9 BRIGADE
Brigadier J.C. Cunningham MC
2 Lincolns: LtCol. C.E. Welby-Everard
1 KOSB: LtCol. G.D. Renny
2 RUR: LtCol. I.C.H. Harris
9 Brigade Defence Platoon

The Reserve Brigade with the East Riding Yeomanry in support was to move initially to concentration areas around Plumetot. The Brigade was mobile with two battalions on bicycles. It was given a number of possible tasks that would be carried out on the order of the Divisional commander. The main task was to move forward and provide right flank protection to 185 Brigade and linking up with the Canadians moving inland from Juno Beach. In the event of 185 Brigade failing to take Caen it was tasked to attack the city from the west.

The 9 Brigade plan instructed 2nd Lincolns to clear the Brigade concentration area south of Lion-sur-Mer and be prepared to take Cresserons and Plumetot. The KOSB and RUR were to then advance to their objectives at St Contest and Malon accompanied and supported by the East Riding Yeomanry.

1ST SPECIAL SERVICE BRIGADE (later 1st Commando Brigade)
Brigadier The Lord Lovat DSO, MC
No. 3 Commando (Army) Lt Col. Peter Young DSO, MC
No. 4 Commando (Army) Lt Col. Robert Dawson
No. 6 Commando (Army) Lt Col. Derek Mills-Roberts DSO, MC
N0. 45 Royal Marine Commando Lt Col. Charles Ries RM

Each Commando consisted of 24 officers and 440 other ranks. The men were divided into troops each of three officers and sixty men.

This included Nos. 1 and 8 French Troops of No. 10 Inter-Allied Commando (under the command of Commandant Philippe Kieffer).

1st Special Service Brigade was to land on Queen Red and execute intermediate missions before linking up with 6th Airborne Division when it would revert under command of General Gale. Its final D-Day objective was to help secure the eastern, seaward, flank of the beachhead in the area of Le Plein, Amfreville and Hauger. A task that the brigade would sustain with reinforcements from 4th Special Service Brigade for over eighty days:

0755 hours No. 4 Commando and Nos. 1 and 8 French Troops were to land and silence the Casino strongpoint and clear Ouistreham, which included destroying the coastal defence battery consisting of six 155mm guns. Once the mission had been executed the Commando would revert under command and rejoin 1st Special Service Brigade.

0840 hours Lovat's brigade headquarters and No. 6 Commando would land and move inland rapidly and link up with unites of 6th Airborne Division at Pegasus Bridge and the cross the canal and river before moving north east and securing the high ground around Amfreville.

0910 hours No. 3 Commando and 45 Royal Marine Commando were to land and support Lovat's operations in Amfreville. In addition, 41 Commando was similarly tasked to clear the coastline to Luc-sur-Mer and then revert under command of 4th Special Service Brigade.

27 (INDEPENDENT) ARMOURED BRIGADE
Brigadier G E Prior Palmer

The 27 Armoured Brigade consisted of three armoured regiments: the 13th/18th Hussars, the Staffordshire Yeomanry, and the East Ridings Yeomanry, under command of Brigadier Eroll Prior-Palmer. The brigade was temporarily attached to 3rd Division for the assault. 13th/18th Royal Hussars (QMO) was in support of 8 Infantry Brigade in the lead echelon with A and B Squadrons in support of the two assault battalions. The third squadron was attached to the Suffolks for their tasks at Periers Ridge. Once individual squadron and regimental task had been achieved the brigade was to concentrate as soon as its individual regiments became available and then support operations on Caen. The Brigade was equipped with 190 Shermans and 33 Stuart light tanks. One unit, the 13th/18th Hussars, would deploy from their LCTs 5,000 yards out to sea and strike out for shore in their unseaworthy Duplex Drive (DD) 'amphibious' Sherman tanks. The other two armoured regiments of 27 Armoured Brigade were both equipped with

Shermans and Stuarts. The brigade numbered 3,400 all ranks and 1,200 vehicles; a sizable addition to the division.

By D+6 the tanks would be retasked east of the Orne to support the defense of the 6th Airborne Bridgehead.

From Plan to Action

After a period of settled weather at the end of May the forecast for 5 June (provisionally selected as D-Day) had deteriorated to such an extent that Eisenhower postponed the invasion by twenty-four hours. At the 2145 hours conference on Sunday 4 June, Group Captain Stagg Chief Meteorological Officer at SHAEF, could announce a period of 'relatively good weather' on 6 June. Eisenhower then said, after some debate with Ramsay, Montgomery, Tedder, Leigh-Mallory, and Bedell Smith:

'Well, I am quite positive we must give the order; the only question is whether we should meet again in the morning. Well I don't like it but there it is. Well boys, there it is, I don't see how we can possibly do anything else.'

Thanks to efforts of the meteorological staff, a short window of opportunity had been identified, enabling the Supreme Allied Commander to launch D-Day on 6 June.

CHAPTER FOUR

THE ASSAULT:
LA BRECHE D'HERMANVILLE – Stand A

"The game's a foot, follow your spirit"
Shakespeare King Henry V

Route to Stand A

From Caen proceed **north on the D515** following directions to Ouistreham Car Ferry. This fast road follows the west bank of the Canal de Caen, also known as the Orne Canal. Note the exit to Benouville and Pegasus Bridge. Proceed **towards Ouistreham Car Ferry** at the **first roundabout** by taking the **right fork** on the **D84**. At the next roundabout note the Comite du Debarquement Monument on the roundabout. Again **follow signs** to the car ferry terminal by driving along the slower canal road. Note the Ouistreham lock gates and beyond, on the far bank, the island promontory of the Pointe du Siege. Identify the dark brown Maginot turret opposite the ferry terminal building. You may wish to **park in the terminal car park** and cross the lock gates, noting that that these gates and the defenses, including the turret, had to be secured by troops landing on Sword Beach on D-Day.

Directly opposite the terminal building main entrance is a memorial to the British Royal Navy and Royal Marine crews who manned over 4,000 landing craft, ships and barges transporting the Allied soldiers and their equipment to Normandy 'or supported them with their guns and rockets, from D-Day, 6 June 1944 until the end of the Second World War in Europe on 8 May 1945.'

Rejoin your transportation and **exit the port** to the **north** past the hotels and restaurants until the road turns west and follows the sand dunes and coastline towards Riva Bella, Colleville Montgomery Plage and Hermanville sur Mer. Five blocks from the ferry terminal on the left will be the Museum of the Atlantic Wall (Le Grand Bunker) identifiable by its 52-foot-high concrete artillery observation tower. The fully restored fortification is the only significant component of the Atlantic Wall remaining in Ouistreham.

Continue on along the coast road **through Riva Bella** noting the post war Casino and Tourist Office (Tel: 02 31 97 18 63) on the right. At the **roundabout keep right** in order to remain on the coast road. After the Casino park and identify the Musee du No 4 Commando on the south side of the road, and on the dunes a memorial to No 4 Commando and Commandant Philippe Kieffer. The memorial is a symbolic flame surmounting a German blockhouse cupola. It was erected in 1984. The Museum opposite contains memorabilia and details of German defenses in the area.

Proceed along the **shore road** and observe how Sword Beach opens out in a wide sweeping crescent. After several hundred meters Riva Bella blends into

Colleville Montgomery Plage. Note the German blockhouse on the left hand side and the NTL post. The blockhouse has been integrated into the flat-roofed three story dark slate fronted house next to it. Note its protected gun port facing along the beach to the west. On the dunes there is a further memorial to the 177 French Commandoes under Kieffer who landed with No. 4 Commando, and No. 3 and 6 Commando and 45 Commando, all units of Lord Lovat's 1st Special Service Brigade.

Turn left at the blockhouse and go to the **junction with D514** and **turn right** (west). At the junction with the D60a note the bronze statue of Montgomery set back from the road in a square and garden. The statue, sculpted by Vivian Mallock, was unveiled 6 June 1996 by Prince Michael of Kent. The statue was presented to Colleville Montgomery by the Normandy Veterans Association (NVA) and the D-Day Normandy Fellowship and matches the statue in Portsmouth that stands outside the D-Day Museum adjacent to Southsea Castle.

Walk across the D514 at the pedestrian crossing and enter Avenue du No 4 Commando and identify two memorials. One marks the site of the first British burials of 6 June 1944 and one to Kieffer's French commandos. Rejoin your transportation and **proceed west** along the **D514**.

Two blocks before the junction with D60b there will be a obvious change of direction to what has been a very straight road. Note the AVRE Churchill tank with its Petard Mortar and **turn off to the right** before passing the tank and park your vehicle in the allocated spaces. Having read the dedication plaque accompanying the tank, a Churchill AVRE of Hobart's 79th Armoured Division placed in La Breche in 1987 by 3rd Armoured Division, and the NTL post, please **walk** along Rue du Docteur Turgis to the small square adjacent to the Hotel de la Mer. **Turn right** and walk towards the beach and note the memorials to the 3rd Division, Royal Navy midget submarines and Royal Artillery.

In the adjacent Syndicat d'Initiative Hermanville sur Mer there is an Exposition Historique de Sword Beach. Having looked at the displayed documents and diorama here please proceed to the beach, sit on the bench to the left of the exit and consider the events that took place around you in the middle part of the last century.

AVRE Churchill tank serving as a present-day memorial at La Breche.

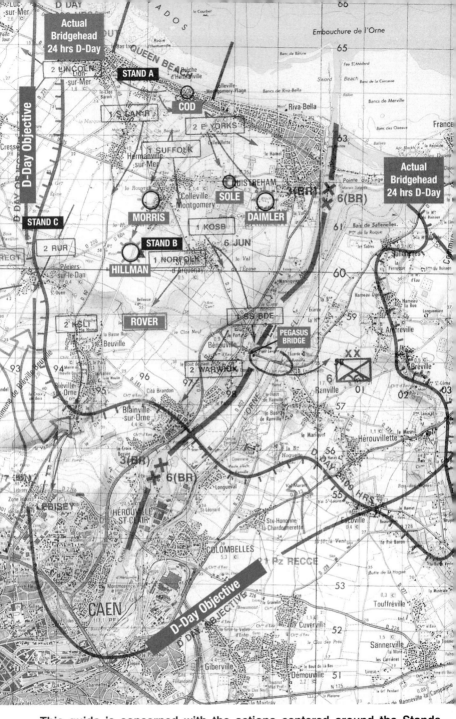

This guide is concerned with the actions centered around the Stands indicated (A, B and C). German strongpoints are indicated under their Allied codenames COD, SOLE, DAIMLER, MORRIS, HILLMAN.

The invasion fleet off the southern coast of England.

The Sea Passage

On 5 June, as the first groups of the NEPTUNE assault force sailed from their sheltered ports in Britain, the assembling Allied fleet learned that Rome had been liberated. Before the day was far advanced, a steady stream of 1,213 warships and 4,126 landing craft was proceeding to sea. As one reporter wrote of this spectacle 'They came, rank after relentless rank, ten lanes wide, twenty miles across, five thousand ships of every description.' For many young men going in to battle for the first time it must have been a rousing and emotional time as their view of home and safety receded with each mile sailed to the south. Officers on board each craft now broke open the sealed map packs and detailed orders for the invasion. Most now learned for the first time that their objective was Normandy. Maps and final orders were issued to commanders and soldiers alike, and weapons cleaned and oiled in final preparation for a cold and fearful landing on a very hostile shore.

By the evening of 5 June the minesweepers had cleared the way through the German sea mine barriers, in spite of heavy seas and strong tides making exact navigation difficult. In mid-Channel a mine-cleared rendezvous had been prepared codenamed 'Piccadilly Circus.' From there, the five landing groups, Forces Utah, Omaha, Gold, Juno, and Sword proceeded towards their objectives. As the early morning progressed the assault troops left the comparative comfort and security of the transports and loaded into their appointed assault craft that were bouncing like corks in a bottle. Many of the soldiers were already weakened by seasickness. Lieutenant IC Dickinson MC of 77 Assault Squadron RE recalled:

> We were up early the next morning, and I for one went straight to the gunwales! The approach was just like the approach on Exercise LEAPYEAR in the Moray Firth. Everything seemed quiet, but soon we could discern the shore, and then it became more and more visible. A destroyer [the Svenner] went down on our port beam. Then we saw flashes on the coast and began to slacken speed.

With a heavy swell and four foot waves the assault troops now faced a long, wet, uncomfortable, and potentially dangerous run-in to the beach. As many soldiers and sailors witnessed (following the sinking of the *Svenner*) with horror during the approach to the hostile shore, the navy crews had been forbidden to stop and pick up survivors if their craft were carrying military personnel (assault troops) or vehicles. Only the designated US Coast Guard Cutters attached to the Allied convoys could be spared to rescue drowning personnel. This was no exercise. Some soldiers struggled and controlled their innermost fears. Major

Approaching the Normandy coast.

HG Jones MC of the 2nd Battalion King's Shropshire Light Infantry (KSLI) wrote in his personal account:

My feelings at this point were that first and foremost I wanted to get off the ship and feel terra firma beneath my feet again. I had no conscious fears about the inevitable battle to come my main fear was that the Germans may have poured oil onto the sea and would set it alight. The thought that I might end up like so many fighter pilots with badly burned, scared faces really did worry me.

At 0550 hours just before dawn on the 6 June gigantic flashes and flickering tongues of flame on the horizon told the assault troops that the bombardment force had commenced the task of engaging the enemy coastal defenses in the Sword sector. Brief duels occurred as German batteries responded. Overhead a great air armada was similarly engaged with its vital air and airborne tasks. The fleet had watched in silence as thousands of aircraft passed overhead throughout the night. No shots were fired. The fleet had been forbidden to engage aircraft during this approach to the continent after the disastrous friendly fire incidents in Sicily the year before. As the naval orders emphatically stated in capital letters:

Bostons of 88 Squadron, 2nd TAF taking off for a sorte over the Normandy beaches.

RAF gliders and their tugs passing over Sword Beach on D-Day.

I HOLD COMMANDING OFFICERS RESPONSIBLE THAT OFFICERS OR RATINGS IN CHARGE OF THE ANTI-AIRCRAFT DEFENCE OF THEIR SHIP, OR OF GUNS, FULLY UNDERSTAND THE ORDERS.

Just as well. As Harry Jones of 2 KSLI recalled: 'Overhead were hundreds of aircraft all heading for the French coast American Flying Fortress bombers, Lightning and Typhoon fighters.'

It was an impressive and encouraging sight. In the final minutes before beaching the assault troops would witness one final air attack by Allied fighter-bombers on the shore defenses and coastal villas that were already shrouded in smoke and the concussion of explosions.

The German concrete emplacements had not been badly damaged by preliminary bombardment and perhaps fortuitously no craters had been blown either in the roads leading off the beaches, or on the roads immediately inland. Surprisingly there were few mines buried on the beach itself. Damage to craft coming in was being caused mainly by mines and shells fixed to the hedgehog obstacles. Thickly sown mines were soon found on the roads immediately behind the dunes, on the roads leading away from the beaches to the main lateral road, and in the narrow lanes between the beachfront houses. Beyond the main lateral road, all minefields were marked and wired, but were found to be mainly dummies consisting of flat metal plates manufactured

Incredible German photograph showing the invasion fleet off the French coast at Lion-sur-Mer, Sword Beach, taken from Merville Plage.

specially for this purpose in Holland. The mines found around the exits from the beaches were chiefly Teller mines, S-mines, and French light anti-tank mines. Picric mines were also found at Luc-sur-Mer. No wooden mines were found at this stage. Electrically controlled 'Beetles' (remote control caterpillar-tracked bombs) had been dug in behind the dunes, but no recorded instance of their use has been found. After being disarmed, they were popular with the sappers as beach runabouts.

Waiting to meet the forces landing at Queen beach were members of 736th Regiment of 716th Coastal Defence Division. It was imperative that 3rd Division, with its supporting tanks from 27 Armoured Brigade, should secure a sizeable bridgehead before the panzers of the 21st Panzer Division, which was positioned at Caen, could intervene. The rapid enlargement of the bridgehead depended on the speed with which troops could be landed and cleared from the beaches, and the clearance of both beach obstacles and beach exits was fundamental to the success of the landing programme.

3rd Division had the capability and engineer resources to make

eight gaps in the coastal defences, and the modern beach exit marks one such gap called Lane 8 or Exit E. The gaps made in the sea wall, wire and obstacles were to be made by assault engineers from 77 and 79 Assault Squadrons. The gaps were then to be exploited by vehicles supporting the two assault battalions: 1 South Lancashires on your immediate right as you face out to sea on Queen White, and 2 East Yorks on Queen Red about 500-800 meters further to your east. To achieve this initial task each infantry assault company would be directly supported by an engineer assault demolition team from 16 Field Engineer Company to clear further gaps and obstacles.

With all the confusion of battle, the division's assault frontage was about 3,000 metres wide reaching from the yellow faced coastal villa on your left (west) and the modern gray slate roofed house to your right (east). This is emphasised so that the reader can appreciate how congested the assault sector could become given the limited exits. A rising tide, abnormally high due to the unseasonable channel storms, would also reduce the beach from a normal thirty metre width at high tide, to a mere ten metres of congested fire-raked sand as the morning progressed.

The Battle for the Beach

By 0530 hours the soldiers were grouped on the boat decks of their LSIs, hove-to at the lowering position. A and B Companies of the 2nd East Yorkshires in addition to A and C Companies of the South Lancashires climbed into their LCAs and were lowered into the heaving sea. Reserve companies and battalion headquarters followed them, and as they headed for the shore past HMS *Largs* a bugler of the East Yorkshires sounded the General Salute, which was acknowledged by the Divisional Commander, Tom Rennie, and Admiral Talbot. Ahead of them, in an LCA carrying A Company headquarters of the East Yorkshires was the legendary second in command of the battalion, Major C K King DSO, known throughout the division as 'Banger.' He held the attention of his men by reading the most inspiring extracts from Shakespeare's King Henry V over the craft's tannoy system. He would be one of the leading infantry across the beach followed by his batman and the assault companies. This inspiring officer was to be killed in action 18 April 1945.

While the infantry could only wait, huddled in their LCAs until the moment of beaching, the gunners following behind were able to fire the 3rd Division's first shells at the enemy since May 1940. Major Hendrie Bruce, battery captain of 9th (Irish) Field Battery, 7th Field Regiment, describes his role and view of the landing:

By this time the big LSIs had hove-to at the lowering position and

Run-in to Queen Beach. Note the bridge layer on the left

had launched the 30-odd LCAs carrying the assault companies of the East Yorkshires and south Lancashires. These small craft were making their way, pitching and rolling, towards the distant shore, which was now clearly visible in the light of a gray stormy day and appeared absolutely deserted. We could see the long row of villas and boarding houses on the sea front and identified the mouth of the River Orne by the lighthouse at Ouistreham but had not positively identified strong point 'Cod' as yet.

Meanwhile the LCTs carrying the DD Tanks of the 13th/18th Royal Hussars and the AVREs of 5th Assault Regt RE kept steaming steadily on. It was planned that the former should heave-to at 7,000 yards and launch the DDs but owing to the heavy sea running they closed to 5,000 yards. We were quite close when some time after 0600 hrs we saw them swing round with their bows down wind and lower their ramps, allowing the extraordinary amphibious tanks with high, inflated bulwarks to crawl down into the water and set off for the shore looking like a lot of rubber dinghies. We were content to cruise along in their wake, scanning the coastline constantly with our special-issue naval binoculars until we were satisfied that we had identified 'Cod.'

We had now closed the shore to about 3,000 yards. Further out to sea came the group of 18 LCTs carrying the divisional artillery and at about 06.3ohrs, when they were about 15,000 yards from the shore, they began to change formation in readiness for the 'run-in-shoot', as it was called. Led by LCT 331 (a troop, 7th Field Regt aboard), the craft adopted an arrowhead formation in three groups of six each with 7th Field Regt in

the centre and 33rd and 76th(Highland) Field Regts slightly to left and right rear respectively in close attendance was a motor launch (ML) equipped with radar to calculate the opening range. The radio links were working perfectly and all was now ready for ranging to being at H-42 at 0644 hours (1 min late) the first ranging rounds were fired by A Troop, 7th Field Regiment a section salvo of white-correction was given and the range, confirmed by the radar ML, passed to the three adjutants at the control sets of the leading craft of their regiments. Monitors, cruisers and destroyers had already begun promptly at H-35 (0650 hours) the seventy-two 105mm and self propelled guns of 3rd Division Artillery opened fire at just over 10,000 yards, firing HE, Rate 3. The field artillery was now playing a unique naval role in the softening-up of the defences by firing from the decks of their LCTs, which maintained a steady speed and course with their bows aimed at the target. The guns had been embarked side by side in sections with 2 guns forward, 2 right aft, and other vehicles in between. Over 100 rounds per gun had been stacked on the tank decks to be expended solely on the run-in: mostly HE but some smoke also, if required. At Rate 3, over 200 rounds per minute were arriving on the target which was seen to be well covered with burst both on the foreshore and among the buildings behind, and by the end of the bombardment some 6,500 rounds, all HE; had been fired. The steady rate of decrease in range was calculated by an instrument called the Coventry Clock with which each GPO, (Gun Position Officer) standing on the bridge of his craft, was equipped, a stream of range corrections, dropping 100 yards at a time, was given out over the tannoy loudspeakers.

The din down in the tank decks was deafening and not only the gunners, but all personneldrivers, signalers, cooks etc were kept busy passing the ammunition and throwing the empty cartridge cases overboard. The 105mm ammunition came packed in large cardboard cylinders and these, floating in their thousands in the wake of the LCTs, laid a clear trail to the beach for those who followed.

The LCTs closed with the shore and his account continues:

The enemy had now wakened up with a vengeance and the sea around the leading craft was peppered with splashes. Several LCTs took evasive action, causing confusion in general and some casualties among the DDs in particular and although many of the splashes could be attributed to enemy fire, some of our own rounds appeared to be falling short. We were particularly concerned at the fact that the pitching of the divisional artillery LCTs in the unusually rough sea might be lengthening the zone of the guns so, as the first assault wave was

*nearing the beach, I gave a correction of 'add 600'. The trouble persisted
on the right of the target so I stopped the 76th to try and sort things out
it was immediately apparent that the culprit was an LCT(R) whose
salvoes of rockets were falling short so I immediately gave 'go on' and
the 76th resumed at an increased rate to catch up. It was now H-5 when
all the guns lifted 400 yards; the assault then went in at 0725 hours, on
time. The run-in-shoot terminated, and my first task of the day was
over.'*

Once the run-in-shoot was completed the LCTs carrying the Priests
turned away from the beach to await their appointed landing time at
about H+195 minutes. As they made their turn they witnessed the first
moments of the assault. Acting Major Robin Dunn (aged 24) was the
commander of 16th Battery, 7th Field Regiment. His memoirs of D-Day
provide a valuable account of events in Normandy:

*'We could just see the turrets of the DD tanks above the waves, with
tracer flying inland from them, and the AVREs crawling up the beach
and little figures running among them, and the hundreds of little
twinkling lights as the air force bombed the various strongpoints.*

*'We turned away to sea after our shoot, passing bobbing assault
landing craft full of steel-helmeted infantry and infantry landing craft
with waving green bereted commandos on board.'*

Amongst the DD tanks was Lance Corporal Hennessey of A Squadron
13th/18th Royal Hussars. He provided a dramatic description of the
DD tank assault on Sword Beach. He was one of the lucky DD crews
that made it to the beach unscathed. Twenty-four DD tanks were successfully launched at 5,000 yards. Of those two would be rammed and
drowned by oncoming LCTs, five would be swamped in the surf
including Hennessey's tank, and a further four damaged by enemy fire
on landing. This would leave thirteen tanks mobile to support the
troops on the beach until the remaining armour could arrive dry-shod
in follow-on waves:

*'We were roused long before dawn on the morning of 6 June. The sea
was still rough and there was a strong wind blowing. We heard and
watched the airborne force pass over us, hosts of gliders following their
tugs, preceded by the aircraft carrying the parachutists and the busy
fighter escorts above them. As daylight slowly appeared we could see
ships of every description stretching away to the horizon on both sides
of us and to the rear. It was a stupendous sight, which must remain in
the memory of all who saw it. We marveled that such a gigantic force
could assemble over a period of five days and move across the English
Channel undetected.*

At last the order came to board the tanks. We climbed on, stowed away bedding rolls and made sure that everything was in its place, and we took post to inflate the screen. The air bottle was turned on and the screen began to rise. We took particular care, this time to make sure that the struts were secure because we could feel the effect those large waves were having on the LCT and we were under no illusions as to what they would do to a puny DD tank once we got into the water.

'The bombardment started with a tremendous roar of gunfire. On our left we heard a terrifying "whooshing" noise and saw a veritable fire-work display as the rocket firing ship, LCT(R) went into action. The burning projectiles carved an arc through the sky as they sped towards the shore. Beyond her stood HMS Warspite, adding a loud contribution from her large guns. We had been warned that it would be very noisy, but this still took us by surprise.

'We heard the order over the ship's tannoy, "down door, no 1", and we knew this was our cue. The ramp on the bow of our LCT was lowered into the sea, the ship hove to, tank engines started, and Sergeant Rattle's tank moved forward down the ramp and nosed into the waves. We followed, and as we righted in the water I could just see the shore line some 5,000 yards away; it seemed a very long distance and in a DD Tank, in that sea, it certainly was!

'Slowly, we began to make headway. The crew were all on deck apart from Harry Bone who was crouched in the driving compartment, intent on keeping the engine running because, as we all knew, if that stopped we stood no chance of survival. The noise seemed to increase and the sea appeared even rougher from this low point of view, with only a flimsy canvas screen between us and the waves. We shipped a certain amount of water over the top of the screen from time to time, so Trooper Joe Gallagher, the co-driver, whose task it was to man the bilge pump, was kept hard at work.

'Each side of us other DD Tanks were launching. To my right and behind me I saw Captain Noel Denny's tank as it came down the ramp and into the sea. It straightened up and began to make way, but behind it I could see the large bulk of its LCT creeping forward. The distance between them closed, and in a very few minutes the inevitable happened. The bows of the LCT struck the DD Tank and forced it under the water. The tank disappeared beneath the LCT and was never seen again. Captain Denny managed to escape and was picked up, the tank was sunk [it sank in 25 feet of water and ended-up upside down] and the rest of the crew was lost. There was nothing anybody could do. It was our first casualty.

Shermans with floatation skirts inflated – not recommended for use in a heavy sea swell!

'We battled on towards the shore through the rough sea. We were buffeted about unmercifully, plunging into the troughs of the waves and somehow wallowing up again to the crests. The wind, fortunately, was behind us, and this helped a little. The noise continued and by now the shells and rockets were passing over our heads, also, we were aware that we were under fire from the shore. The Germans had woken up to the fact that they were under attack and had brought their own guns into action. It was a struggle to keep the tank on course, but gradually the shoreline became more distinct and before long we could see the line of houses, which were our targets. Seasickness was now forgotten. It took over an hour of hard work to reach the beach and it was a miracle that most of us did. As we approached, we felt the tracks meet the shelving sand of the shore, and slowly we began to rise out of the water. We took post to deflate the screen, one man standing to each strut. When the base of the screen was clear of the water, the struts were broken, the air released and the screen collapsed. We leapt into the tank and were ready for action.

'"75, HE, action-traverse right, steady, on. 300 white fronted house first floor window, centre". "On". "Fire!" within a minute of dropping our screen we had fired our first shot in anger. There was a puff of smoke and brick dust from the house we had aimed at, and we continued to engage our targets. Other DD Tanks were coming in on both sides of us and by now we were under enemy fire from several positions, which we identified and to which we replied with 75mm and Browning machine gun fire. The beach, which had been practically deserted when we had arrived, was beginning to fill up fast. The infantry were wading through the surf and advancing against a hail of small arms fire and mortar bombs. We gave covering fire wherever we could, and all the time the build-up of men and vehicles continued.

'Harry Bone's voice came over the intercom "lets move up the beach a bit I'm getting bloody wet down here!" We had landed on a fast incoming tide, so the longer we stood still the deeper the water became. As we had dropped our screen, the sea was beginning to come in over the top of the driver's hatch and by now he was sitting in a pool of water. The problem was that the promised mine clearance had not yet taken place so we had to decide whether to press on through a known mine field, or wait until a path had been cleared and marked.

'Suddenly, the problem was solved for us. One particularly large wave broke over the stern of the tank and swamped the engine, which spluttered to a halt. Now, with power gone, we could not move, even if we wanted to. Harry Bone and Joe Gallagher emerged from the driving compartment, soaking wet and swearing.

'More infantry were coming ashore, their small landing craft driving past us and up to the edge of the beach. There was quite a heavy firefight in progress so we kept our guns going for as long as possible,

Approaching Queen Red. The two houses on the right help identify the exact spot today.

but the water in the tank was getting deeper and we were becoming flooded. At last we had to give up. We took out the browning machine guns and several cases of .3 inch belted ammunition, inflated the rubber dinghy and, using the map boards as paddles, began to make our way to the beach. We had not gone far when a burst of machine gun fire hit us. Gallagher received a bullet in the ankle, the dinghy collapsed and turned over, and we were all tumbled into the sea, losing our guns and ammunition.

'Somehow, we managed to drag Gallagher and ourselves ashore. We got clear of the water and collapsed onto the sand, soaking wet cold and shivering. A DD tank drove up and stopped beside with Sergeant Hepper grinning at us out of the turret "can't stop!" he said, and threw us a tin can. It was a self-heating tin of soup, one of the emergency rations with which we had been issued. One pulled a ring on top of the tin, and miraculously it started to heat itself up. We were very grateful for this, and as we lay there on the sand, in the middle of the battle taking turns to swig down the hot soup, we were approached by an irate captain of Royal Engineers who said to me: "get up, corporal – that is no way to win the second front!" he was absolutely right of course. Rather shame-facedly we got up, moved further up the beach and found some medical orderlies into whose care we delivered Joe Gallagher who cheered up considerably when someone told him he would be returning

to Blighty as a wounded "D-Day hero". We left him at the field dressing station and moved on. We had only our pistols with us, but we found a discarded Sten gun and some magazines. Attaching ourselves to a section of the South Lancashire's, we made our way in-land. The beach, by now, was a very unhealthy place to be, it was under intensive small arms and mortar fire, mines were exploding and being detonated by our own mine clearance services, and all the time the build-up of troops and vehicles continued, making it a very crowded area. Clearly, we were not of much use to the infantry in our un-armed state, so I found the Royal Navy beach master and reported our presence to him. He was a very busy man at the time, and advised me to: "get off my bloody beach!" We made our way to the road which ran parallel to the sea, some four of five hundred yards inland, and there we met up with some other un-horsed tank crews.

'We could not help feeling a bit unwanted at that stage. There was plenty of action taking place, but there was not a lot that we could do to influence the course of the battle and nobody seemed keen to invite us to join in. of course, we had already played our part, and we could look back with some satisfaction. We had done what most people had thought was impossible, we had swum a thirty-two ton tank through 5,000 yards of savagely rough sea and had given that vital support to the infantry to enable them now to have the chance to do their job of clearing the beach. On reflection, I had learned a valuable lesson from the events of that morning. Sergeant Hepper, for instance, had clearly not been deterred by the prospect of mines on the beach and had driven his tank shore, accepting the risk. If I had used initiative and done the same, our tank would not now be standing submerged some 150 yards out in the sea. The RE Captain too, had the right idea of "press on, regardless". In the heat of battle it really does not pay to sit back and weigh up the pros and cons of a situation, it is quick decision and immediate action which brings results. I mentioned these thoughts to Harry Bone, whose only comment was: "Bugger that! If we had hit a mine, I would have been sitting right on top of it."

The beach was still a scene of frantic activity. Landing craft were coming in, depositing their loads of men and vehicles, then backing out to sea again. The area was swept by machine gun and mortar fire and snipers were busy from the windows of the houses. Shells and mortars were kicking up clouds of sand, the noise level remained very high, and the infantry were taking a lot of casualties. I saw death for the first time that day, and also for the first time I came face to face with the German Army. About two dozen prisoners were being marched to the beach,

DD and Engineer tanks on the beach.

hands held aloft some were wounded, all looked shocked and frightened. They were a scruffy crowd, not at all the 'supermen' we had been led to believe were opposing us. Most professed to be white Russians or Poles, but there were a few who were arrogantly German. Eventually, we were found by Major Wormald who directed us to make our way to the village of Hermanville. We were delighted to see him and to know that he had survived the landings. As he drove off in his tank, we felt a return of confidence as we started the three-mile trek to Hermanville.'

The carefully choreographed plan was to being affected by the sea state; this meant that the DD tanks, assault engineers and leading infantry companies of the East Yorkshires and South Lancashires were now sweeping towards the shore together. Major AR Rouse, of the South Lancashires (in 8 Brigade's first wave) described the first desperate minutes of the 3rd Division's landing:

'The boat crews had been ordered to go in at four knots and hit the beach hard. During the last 100 yards of the run-in everything seemed to happen at once. Out of the haze of smoke the underwater obstacles loomed up. We had studied them on air photographs and knew exactly what to expect but somehow we had never realised the vertical height of them, and as we weaved in between iron rails and ramps and pickets with teller mines on top, like gigantic mushrooms we seemed to be groping through a grotesque petrified forest the noise was so continuous that it seemed almost like a siren. The seamanship was magnificent. The LCAs weaved in and out of the obstacles and we almost had a dry landing. I have very little recollection of wading ashore; there was too

99

much going on above and around to notice it. It was, however, apparent from the beginning that it was by no means an unopposed landing. Mortar fire was coming down on the sands, an 88 mm gun was firing along in the line of the beach and there was continuous machine gun and rifle fire. Immediately ahead of us a DD Tank, its rear end enveloped in flames, unable to get off the beach, continued to fire its guns.'

In planning his battalion's assault the commanding officer of the South Lancashires, Lieutenant Colonel Richard Burbury, had tried to visualise some of the difficulties of command and control during the first chaotic moments of the initial assault. To ease his task he had a hand flag made in the battalion colours to help his men identify him. The idea was that this would be a rallying symbol and he could be easily identified. He carried this in his hand as he landed. Unfortunately it made him far too conspicuous and one of the enemy defenders killed him as he reached the beach wire. The second in command, Major Jack Stone, took over command – but not the flag.

Because of the heavy swell A and C Companies had actually landed almost simultaneously with the leading DD Tanks. This mixed force immediately came under heavy fire. Major Harwood, commanding A Company was fatally wounded. One of his platoon commanders was also killed while crossing the beach. Lieutenant Pierce took command of the company and moved off to the west clearing a series of fortified houses. He was later wounded and before their task had been completed the company was left with only one officer.

The men of C Company were more fortunate, they crossed the beach with only light casualties and Major Eric Johnson directed them to the east towards strong point Cod also known to the assault troops as Strongpoint 0880 after its map square grid reference. The follow up second echelon companies were to have landed exactly behind the lead companies but in the confusion of smoke and battle they hit the beach well to the east with battalion headquarters almost exactly opposite the western end of Cod. Major Harrison, B company commander was killed immediately and one of his subalterns, Lieutenant Bell-Walker took command. He moved a platoon to the left to attack a concrete pillbox, which was firing from an defilade position with devastating effect along the beach. Bell-Walker's actions were witnessed as he attacked the bunker, in what was described later as classic battle school fashion. He crept round behind the position threw a grenade through a gun slit and then gave the interior a burst of Sten gun fire. He was killed instantly by a burst of machine-gun fire from one of Strongpoint Cod's depth positions. By his action he had, however, opened a way for

The Assault area:
Queen Red, 2 E.Yorks; Queen White, 1 S. Lanc Reg.

the rest of his company to get off the beach. They had landed almost exactly opposite the strongest fortifications of Cod itself, and rather like the Americans to the west on Omaha Beach, these troops were immediately committed in a frontal attack.

Lieutenant KP Baxter of the 2nd Battalion the Middlesex Regiment landed on Sword Beach with responsibility for the coordinated development of beach exits in his area. His account is rich in detailed observations:

'We could see nothing beyond a horizon of water. Many of us found ourselves mentally checking that the sky was lightening on the port side, showing that we were indeed running south and not back on to an English beach on yet another exercise. The run-in was long, and gradually, in dispersing gloom, we found ourselves joined by more and more craft whilst from the shore started a crescendo of explosions as the air bombardment carpeted the defences.

'It was now getting quite light and we suddenly came upon the midget submarine X.23, a complete surprise to us as it should have been, and we knew nothing of the long vigil that it had kept awaiting our arrival.

'The shoreline became more distinct, but detailed recognition was still impossible due to the heavy pall of smoke and dust still obscuring the buildings. Stabbing orange flames showed the strike of both artillery and the naval bombardment that had now joined in and then suddenly

101

the air was torn with an ear-splitting roar as the rocket ships loose their projectiles. Then we saw the first setback: a returning LCT with her ramp seemingly jammed in the half-lowered position. These craft, four to each beach, carried the specially equipped AVRE. Tanks that were to work in groups of three, the centre tank being armed with a 'snake', a 60-foot long heavy tube of explosive to be pushed through the beach defences and detonated.

Not only would this breach the wire but the explosion was calculated to set off any mines in the near vicinity it would then be the job of the exit teams to clear and widen the corridors by hand and then to signal in following craft as the exits became operative. That one of these AVRE carrying craft had been unable to land its tanks meant that at least one of the beach teams would have to make its exit the hard way.

Steadily the flotilla of LCAs pressed onwards towards the beach. Four hundred yards from the shoreline and the royal marine frogmen slipped over the side to start the job of clearing underwater obstacles. This would be sufficiently hazardous at the best of times, but add to it the risk from all those churning propellers with many more following and their task became most unenviable.

'Closing to the shore rapidly, eyes scanned the clearing haze for familiar landmarks. There were none. A burst of machine-gun fire uncomfortably close overhead brought curses up on those in following craft for their enthusiastic "covering fire". Suddenly a burst ricocheted off the front of the craft, telling us that this was no covering fire. The opposition was very much alive and well.

'We had still been unable to identify our position but we were by now right on top of the beach. The protective steel doors in the bows were opened and everyone waited, tensed for the soft lurching bump. "Ramp down!" and out into knee-deep water.

Baxter then described the assault on Strongpoint Cod. Cod was located at the junction of two beach areas and extended for 400 meters into Queen Red and about 100 meters into Queen White. It actually consisted of twenty separate strongpoints within wire obstacles and interconnecting trenches. This defensive hedgehog comprised of a 75-mm gun; two 50-mm anti-tank guns; three 81-mm mortars; a 37-mm gun and five other machine gun posts each in turn equipped with two or three guns. Forward observation posts and shelters completed a formidable defensive area that would take over three hours to clear and cost the assaulting battalions dearly. It would take the combined efforts of the East Yorks and South Lancashires and supporting tanks and infantry from the No.5 Beach Group (5th Battalion Kings Regiment)

QUEEN WHITE

QUEEN RED

Twin Villas

Trenches

← Lion Sur Mer

Ouistreham →

Strongpoint Cod.Note zig zag pattern of trenches and evidence of aerial bombing.

and No.4 Commando to overwhelm German resistance.

'Ahead, a line of prone figures just above the water's edge and some 200 yards beyond a tank was nosed up against the small strip of dunes at the head of the beach. The first impression was – that the tank had got in ahead of the first wave and they, following the same instructions as given to the beach exit teams, were holding back until the explosive charges had been detonated.

'I had not gone far when I was tripped by some underwater wire and, with no hope of retaining balance with the heavy assault jacket and pack that had been issued to us, went flat on my face. Attempting to rise, I was struck a heavy blow on the back, which flattened me again. Then suddenly the machine gun opened up on us once again. The fire came from dead ahead and we could now make out the shape of a heavy embrasure in the low silhouette of some concrete fortifications at the top of the beach. We then realized that, by the narrowest of margins, we had landed immediately in front of: strong point 0880, codeword Cod.

'Both mortar and light artillery defensive fire was being brought down by the enemy in front of the strong point which now intensified, and a still unspotted machine-gun made an instant target of anything that moved. The prone figures that had first been seen just above the water's edge, we found to be casualties from the leading craft. Our wireless communication had been lost when the corporal operator,

Men belonging to Intermediate Brigade HQ Staff wade ashore from their LSI.

German machine-gunners in defensive positions on the French coast.

corporal Roulier, had been hit on leaving our craft, but on White Beach to our right, troops could be seen crossing the beach and reaching the top. There was a brief lull in the firing and we immediately took this opportunity to make a dash for the top of the beach. Briefly seeking cover behind the motionless tank to count heads, it was found that only the signalman of our group had managed to come through unscathed.

'We had hardly jettisoned our heavy equipment when the strong point above our heads sprang to life once more. German stick grenades somersaulted through the air, their effects being greatly reduced in the soft sand, whilst we in turn desperately sought grenades from amongst the remnants of other detachments now grouping with us. However, further action was promptly eclipsed by the arrival of lieutenant Tony Milne with his machine-gun platoon of the 2nd Battalion Middlesex Regiment. The platoon was equipped with universal carriers, having the heavy Vickers mounted above the engine casing, and were the first infantry fighting vehicles to land.

'Without a moment's hesitation, waterproofing shields were ripped away, gun clamps freed and the leading carrier drove straight at the trench line above our heads with a long swinging traverse from the Vickers, depressing into the trench as they closed. a brief pause silence then at the end of the trench system some fifteen survivors appeared in hasty surrender. Strong point Cod had been taken.

Sheltering from fire on Sword Beach while regrouping after landing.

'A first-aid post was quickly established in the concrete emplacement of the strong point, and then every hand was turned to helping vehicles through the soft sand above the high-water mark. The self-propelled guns of the 76th and 23rd Field Regiments, together with the Royal Marine artillery would be coming in at about 0900 hours[1000 hours after local variations] *and were indeed to establish their first gun line on the water's edge. Already it seemed that we had been there all day.'*

Apart from the depth positions at strongpoint Cod that were still resisting (finally secured at about 1000 hours), 8 Brigade had cleared the immediate beach area of enemy as early as 0810-0830 hours. Within another half an hour elements of the South Lancashires had pushed south and secured Hermanville, while A Company had turned west towards Lion sur Mer to take on strongpoint Trout at the western end of Queen Green. Meanwhile infantry from the East Yorks had started to move east towards strongpoint Sole. As this was taking place the Suffolks were landing in good order and were striking south to their battalion assembly area before enlarging the beachhead; all this within the first hours of landing. Richard Harris was a young infantryman coming ashore with the Suffolks. He recalled:

'Nearer and nearer we drew to the shore...Trembling, my rifle tightly clenched, I crouched awaiting the dreaded shout, "Ramps down!" We

seemed to inch in, in between craft already beached, some of which were burning. The diesels went into reverse, the bows ground into the sand and pebbles and we came to a standstill. "Ramps down!" This was it, I was determined to present myself for the minimum time as a target at the top of the ramp and being one of the first to go I had a clear run.'

The relief of reaching terra firma was quickly overwhelmed by other emotions as the reality of war struck these young men most forcibly. Harris remembered:

'A complete shambles... Against a backdrop of smoke, gutted blazing buildings were several burning knocked out DD tanks and strewn about from the water's edge to the seawall were sodden khaki bundles staining red the sand where they lay. The thought that for them the day was already done appalled me.'

While his assault troops were fighting there way ashore, General Tom Rennie was observing operations from HMS *Largs* and assessing the proper moment at which to land and follow the assault brigades ashore. Captain AC Duckworth RN was at the time Staff Officer (Plans) to Admiral Talbot. He remembered that the GOC was a great inspiration to them all, and recalled that at the time of the landing Rennie and Talbot were on the bridge, and were engaged in a heated argument as to when the General should be allowed to land: Rennie insisted that he should embark in a landing craft forthwith, while

Infantry holding strongpoints along the invasion front put up a strong resistance against the invaders.

Queen White looking East. No.84 Field Company ashore at 0815 hrs.

Talbot stated firmly that he was in command and the general would land at his discretion. Meanwhile, the Norwegian destroyer *Svenner* had been sunk on the port bow by a German E-Boat, and the spread of the incoming torpedoes had narrowly missed sinking HMS *Largs* while this frustrating argument continued. Fortunately, the Captain of HMS *Largs* had taken the necessary avoiding action and Rennie was allowed to land shortly afterwards at 1030 hours. Thus Headquarters 3rd Infantry Division re-established itself in France. Once ashore Rennie was to spend much of the day racing from one critical point to another encouraging and cajoling commanders at every level to 'Drive On.'

Royal Engineer Operations on D-Day

While the infantry and DD Tanks had been overcoming the enemy beach defences the tide, much increased in height by the strong wind, was rapidly covering the sand and beach obstacles behind them and it was now time for the engineer gapping parties to clear gaps and exits from the beach area. The sappers had already suffered heavily from enemy fire; several had been drowned while working on the half submerged beach obstacles. The Commanding Officer of the 5th Assault Regiment, Lieutenant Colonel ABDB Cocks attached from 79th

Armoured Division, had also been killed while disembarking from a LCT, but the work went ahead. On D-Day 5 ARRE would suffer 117 casualties while 22nd Dragoons would have forty-two casualties. Fifteen of their twenty-six Sherman flails alone were knocked out or damaged that day.

For the engineer clearance teams the first priority was the removal or destruction of explosive charges on top of the beach obstacles to create cleared lanes for the follow up waves. Army engineers were tasked to clear these obstacles above and below the high water mark. As Lieutenant IC Dickinson MC explained:

'Obstacles from a depth of ten feet to four feet six inches were the responsibility of the Landing Craft Obstacle Clearance Units of the Royal Navy, and those from four feet six inches to 0 feet were a sapper responsibility. Each Beach White and Red, was allotted five AVREs for obstacle clearance. Our latest information before leaving was that the obstacles were laid in four rows in the following order from the dunes to the sea: two rows of Hedgehogs, Stakes, and Ramped Stakes.

'The intention was to land with the tide lapping the bottom of the ramped stakes. We were to through these, drop our porpoises (waterproofed steel sledges carrying ammunition and explosives) on the beach, and then return, remove such mines as we found on the ramped *stakes and then either run them down or tow them away. Having completed row c we were to go to b, and so on.'*

The sappers had devised and practiced various methods to complete their tasks including the use of fitted slings on their vehicles for towing away the stakes, and waterproofed explosive charges for blowing more difficult obstacles. Unfortunately their well-practiced drills were hampered by the un-seasonal tide, heavy swell and sapper casualties caused by enemy action. Sappers were witnessed swimming out to the obstacles in order to cut away the lethal mines and shells and drop them into the deepening water. Others used a flail tank as a platform to drive between stakes and cut away Tellermines. Many brave men drowned trying to complete their allotted tasks. The conditions for the beach gapping teams were just as grim. Captain A Low of No.2 Troop commanded a beach gapping team and he recalled the effects of enemy small arms fire on the LCT bridge, making it a very unhealthy place for crew and engineer officers alike. On landing, he witnessed one of his tank crews using their flail to pulverise a particularly active German gun position. Tank crews used their vehicle weapons and even small arms to engage, suppress or kill German defenders who exposed themselves in their haste to engaged the men struggling ashore. After supervising the creation of gaps off the beach, Low realised that a knocked-out Sherman tank was blocking one of the vital exits so he used his tank to clear the obstacle in the desperate race against tide and landing schedules.

Meanwhile 246 Field Company had cleared an exit on the right but on the left, where roads were blocked by damaged tanks, it took nearly two hours to open up further exits. To get clear of the beach, vehicles had to move laterally to the west before meeting the road to Hermanville that formed the nearest causeway over the flooded and now marshy land immediately behind the dunes. As the morning progressed, queues at the exits built up, while more and more vehicles were landing on the ever-decreasing strip of sand. The congestion was extremely serious and would ultimately impact on the mission to reach Caen on D-Day. In addition to vehicles waiting to move forward there were now some fifty SP guns (the Priests) firing from the beachand eventually these were standing in the surf. At midday it was decided to suspend beaching for half an hour to allow the congestion to subside.

The armoured engineers of 5th Assault Regiment reinforced the divisional engineers. The engineers were organised into eight gapping teams with additional dismounted sappers from 629 Field Squadron and support teams for the assaulting infantry battalions, consisting of

Queen White Beach during the landings – Lanes have been cleared by 77th Assault Squadron RE.

assault demolition teams and mine clearance teams with each of the assault companies. The gapping teams all succeeded in disembarking with the exception of one LCT carrying the left hand gapping team for Queen White beach. This craft came under close anti-tank gunfire and only the leading flail was beached. The second flail was hit and jammed at the ramp door whilst a hit on a Bangalore torpedo caused an explosion on board. It was at this point that CRE 5th Assault Regiment, in command of all beach clearance and gapping teams, was killed on this craft. Despite heavy casualties to tanks, the gapping teams succeeded in opening four exits within an hour on Queen White beach and in interconnecting them inland, on Queen Red further to the east, teams suffered from heavy enemy fire and to a great extent were reduced to clearance by hand. Damaged tanks blocked their first two exits. One gap with lateral communications was open at H+90 minutes followed by two more within a quarter of an hour.

This notable account is from Sergeant T R Kilvert (a relative of the author) who landed on Queen White beach commanding his AVRE in 1 Troop, 77 Assault Squadron:

'We stood to at dawn on board the LCT 100A at 0500 hours. Breakfast was on but nobody really wanted it, being more or less seasick. I had AVRE 1c started up, all guns loaded and a last minute check over the tank. It was now about 0610 hours and the coastline stood out in the

111

A drowned DD Sherman on Sword Beach.

haze; we were coming in fast. About half a mile out everyone mounted their tanks. Almost in, 400 yards to go when 1c had a violent shake, we had been hit. Damage not known because the LCT had also sustained damage a bit forward and we had to get off at once.

'The LCT stopped:... going down the ramp now and the water was almost up to our cupola. Again we were hit but on our Bobbin, it being at a crazy angle. Coming up out of the water, hit again and at last dry and following 1a up to sand. Hit a mine, one bogie gone, but, following on in 1a's track, we were ordered to put up a windsock, 1a having lost his. Struck a second mine, two bogies and left track gone.

'L/Corporal Fairlie and Sapper Vaughan jumped out to put up a windsock. L/Corporal Fairlie was blown up by a mine as he came round the tank. I ordered abandon tank, take all arms, and jumped out myself, destroyed 'slidex and code papers'. We were all out now petrol was pouring out of 1c and filling the mine crater. Everyone lay down whilst I looked for the L/Corporal's remains. None found so I returned and organised the crew into a fighting patrol. Just then L/Sergeant Freer from 3 Troop joined us; he had swum ashore from his tank which had been on our LCT. Moving up the beach we passed Captain McLennan in 1a, stood on the gap top. I ordered a defensive position and to consolidate in front of 1a on the crossroads.

'Asking the troop leader to cover us, we moved forward behind the leading flail, until he reported no more mines in the road ahead. Again we consolidated. I went back to the beach to bring up the troop. Captain McLennan had now advanced through the gap and was followed by 1b, who stood at the exit a little to one side. I collected L/Sergeant Freer's crew and a couple of infantrymen and brought them forward to our advanced position.

'Again we moved forward (we thought) until a bend in the road cut them, by 1a and 1b from view.

'We advanced in short bounds to the high wall of the large farm.

Here we split into three parties, one covering the main road or killing zone, another as rear protection and another as house clearance.

'It was then that fire came at us from three sides, but bursts from our two Brens brought a lull. Shooting open the garden door, I advanced covered by my L/Sergeant and Sappers Lewis and Hand, up the two paths and raked the whole front of the house and part of the farm with fire killing, we later found eleven of the enemy.

'We rushed the house with hand grenades, and searched it from top to bottom. Going out into the yard we found the air raid shelter and the civilian occupants of the farm.

'Sapper Hand, who spoke the lingo, obtained the information that the big house (on the corner of Hermanville itself) housed about 200 of the enemy I then reorganised the party, sending two runners back to Captain McLennan. Using the road ditch and the garden wall as vantage points we advanced about sixty yards when Sapper Vaughan opened fire with a Sten gun on an enemy party coming down the road towards us. Immediately everyone of us opened fire, and with the two Sergeants with 100 round magazines with their Bren guns this scattered the enemy. An SP gun then came up, followed shortly after by the infantry and Lieutenant Tennent on foot. We then handed over to a RA major, and moved to our RV in a field opposite. On Captain McLennan's instructions we used a detector and tested for mines.

Sergeant Kilvert survived the war. Sadly Captain McLennan was killed on the afternoon of D-Day leading three AVREs in support of No.41 RM Commando in the clearance of German defenses in Lion sur Mer. A German 50mm gun destroyed each of the tanks in turn. A grenade killed McLennan while he was attempting to evacuate his men under cover of a smoke screen and commando supporting fire. He was one of the ten men from 77 Assault Squadron killed on D-Day a further twelve men were wounded. Of the Squadron's armour, three AVREs were destroyed, three were damaged and five were still operational. Two flails had also been lost on the Squadron front. For their work on D-Day, 77 and 79 Assault Squadron personnel were awarded two DSOs, four MCs, and three MMs.

253 Field Company one of 3rd Division's integral sapper companies, was landing with 185 Infantry Brigade and this account gives a clear image of the state of the beaches by the time the Intermediate Brigade started to come ashore:

'Soon I could pick out the silhouette of houses on the low flat skyline and I tried to identify the house with a tower which showed on my panorama this was Lion sur Mer. It was my responsibility to get all

A Sherman Flail knocked out on the beach.

these men and their vehicles clear of the beaches, but from where I was standing on the bridge of this LCT emblazoned with the red and black triangle of 3rd Division. I could not see enough room on the beach for a dinghy to pull in. However, to my intense relief our skipper touched down perfectly full marks to the Royal Navy as he dropped his ramp without mishap just at this moment a shell landed forward on our immediate neighbour and removed his ramp before he reached the beach, and I saw a sapper jump for it and swim loaded like a Christmas tree with assault jerkin and mine detector.

'Now I began to get very impatient because although our ramp was down there was so much traffic in front of the mouth of our craft that none of our vehicles could move. Visions of another shell hitting us amidships and cooking our goose! So I walked off the craft and trudged along the beach to see what the hold up was.

'I never found the cause of this stoppages, but slowly things began to move, terribly slowly it seemed to me; occasionally over the din of the shelling I heard the unmistakable 'woomph' of a mine going off and a stretcher passed me with a badly wounded man with his face knocked about and I realised with a jolt that this was the real thing again. When I had walked as far as the road behind the beach, I saw that mines in the verges had already taken their toll and went back along the column warning every driver including my own, to stick to the crown of the road; then I got aboard and we drove off the beach in a column that was still bonnet to tail.

'This movement was very short lived, for soon there was another

inexplicable hold up and again I got out and walked forward to try to clear the block this time I got as far as the crossroads which lead to Hermanville and as I walked back one of my hussar friends shouted "your truck's had it, sir". It had two rear wheels blown clean away and the centre of the truck ripped up like so much paper-there were seven men aboard but only one was wounded and that not serious, and the track marks of dozens of trucks had crossed this mine before us.

The contents of the truck were vital and included two wireless sets the company control and the rear link to the CRE. We all got busy and unloaded the essentials on to the dusty road in a matter of minutes. How to get all this to our RV was my next problem!'

By nightfall the specialised armour attached to Rennie's division from the 79th Armoured Division and the other engineers from 5th Assault Regiment had helped establish the beachhead.

Expanding the Beachhead

Meanwhile offshore the principal concern for Rear Admiral Talbot remained threat posed by the massive Le Havre battery that could fire directly into the Sword landing area. Heavy smoke screens were laid all morning to prevent the Germans ranging. Instead the battery seemed to be content with shelling the warships. Led by HMS *Warspite*, the warships fired heavy salvos back and kept the Germans occupied.

The pre-assault bombardment by the twenty-two ships of the Bombarding Force and the Allied air forces suffered from the inevitable lack of visibility once the battle started. According to one official report, not all the bombs landed on target. As one officer wrote later he thought that the air bombardment was placed rather too far to the westward, but it was difficult to judge through the smoke and dust as approaching craft reported that they could not recognize the beaches from a distance once the bombardment had commenced.

'The early waves, however, saw all they needed and all spoke highly of the value of the models and photographs, which they were shown in the Commercial Buildings, Portsmouth, prior to sailing. I was surprised to see several houses on the front in Queen sector undamaged and with windows still intact in spite of the bombardment.'

The assault started off with some style. Brigadier the Lord Lovat led his commandos in with the now legendary Piper Bill Millin playing highland reels on the fo'c'sle of his landing craft. The men needed to keep their morale high; many had been on the point of physical and nervous exhaustion after the rough crossing. As one naval officer wryly commented, 'the military were mostly sea-sick.' According to at least one report this was not a universal experience:

'At 0635 I was lowered in LCA 796 from LSI SS Empire Broadsword with thirty men and a captain of the Suffolk regiment. We formed up and left the lowering position at approximately 0645, commencing the run in to White Beach, Sword area, to touch down at H plus 60. The sea was fairly rough but the soldiers, with one or two exceptions, enjoyed the run in.

'At just over 1,000 yards, I signaled all craft to increase to maximum revolutions, and, regardless of our own barrage, some of which fell in our midst, the flotilla hit the beach at full speed, LCT 947 touching down at 0726. Just after the first tank had got ashore from LCT 947, we were hit forward by mortar fire, which exploded the bangalore torpedoes. The second tank (flail) was put out of action, also the tank astern of it. Three army personnel were killed, including the colonel, and seven others wounded.

In spite of some heavy losses of armour, enough flails, DD and AVREs crawled up from the sea to support the individual infantry assaults that would overwhelm the seafront strong points and machine-gun positions. The men of the 8 Infantry Brigade slowly fought their way up onto the promenade and began a series of vicious little close quarter battles for the control of the coastal road and the beachfront villas. Dennis Glover commanded one of the craft carrying Lovat's Commandos. He later reproduced this very personal and vivid account of the assault:

'Now eyes for everything eyes for nothing. The beach looms close, maybe a mile. There are people running up and down it. There are fires, and the bursting of shells down it. Yes, and wrecked landing craft everywhere, a flurry of propellers in the savage surf among the wicked obstructions. Beach clearance parties I expect bloody heroes, every one. Craft stooging quietly in, some of them on fire though. Diesel fuel burns black. That vicious destroyer is irritating me, but the colonel doesn't seem to mind. He's cool, but I'll bet he's worried. Curious how all these soldiers dislike assault by water. I'd hate to dash out of foxholes at machine-guns. Damn him, I can pretend I'm cool too. Starboard ten! It's the noisiest gun in the navy that 4.7-midships cox'n. What a cool disinterested reply he makes. Colonel, you make me grin. I like your nerve.

'We are on those bristling stakes. They stretch before us in rows. The mines on them look as big as planets. And those gray nose shells

1st Special Service Brigade (Commandos) approaching Queen Red Beach at 0845.

pointing towards us on some of them look like beer bottles. Oh God, I would be blown up on a mine like a beer bottle. Whang here it comes those whizzing ones will be mortars and the stuff is falling all round us. Can't avoid them, but the mines and collisions I can avoid.

Speed, more speed. Put them off by speed, weave in and out of those bloody spikes, avoid the mines, avoid our friends, avoid wrecked craft and vehicles in the rising water and get those troops ashore. Everything is working as we've exercised it for so long. Oh hell, this new tin hat is

1st Special Service Brigade (Commandos) ramp going down...

1st Special Service Brigade (Commandos): Piper Bill Millin is close-up and the commander, Lord Lovatt, is the detached figure on the right wading ashore (close to Millin's left arm). Time: H+1.

far too big for me I'll shake it off my head with fright, if I'm not careful.

'Slow ahead together.' slow down to steady the ship, point her as you want her, then half ahead together and on to the beach with a gathering rush. Put her ashore and be damned! She's touched down. One more good shove ahead to wedge her firm. Smooth work! "Now off you go! Good luck, commandos, go like hell! Next meeting Brighton!" how efficiently, how quickly they run down the accustomed ramps, not a man hit that I can see, and there they go, splashing through a hundred yards of water, up over more of the flat beach than that and out of sight among the deadly dunes. The colonel turns to wave and is gone with

them. They ignore the beach fire. They have their objective and they are going for it.'

This was part of the landing of No.6 Commando, its objective, Ouistreham. Meanwhile No.4 Commando had landed earlier than the rest of the brigade, its vital mission being to push inland rapidly and link up with the hard-pressed men of the 6th Airborne Division holding the bridges over the Orne. The rest of the brigade had the difficult task of prizing the Germans out of their heavily fortified positions at Riva Bella and Ouistreham. The port marked the entrance to the river Orne and the lock gates controlling the Caen ship canal. In an ironic twist of history the local inhabitants had set up a monument to their successful repulse of a British attempted landing on 12 July, 1792. Now they were waiting to welcome the British as liberators and, to the great joy of the French inhabitants of Ouistreham and Riva Bella, the new liberators included a Free-French Commando Company under Commandant Kieffer. Villa by villa the commandos shot it out with the Germans until the guns of the Riva Bella casino strongpoint halted them. Kieffer obtained the support of a single DD Tank and by 0930 he had stormed and cleared the casino.

Captain J H Patterson RAMC was attached to No.4 Commando. Lovat quoted his memories of D-Day in his book *March Past*. Again, this account steps back from the 'glory' of D-Day and describes the reality of opposed amphibious assaults where the invader must face not only a prepared enemy in defence but also the hazards of the environment:

'There was thick smoke over the beach, and the tide low but flooding. There were many bodies in the water; one was hanging round one of the tripod obstacles. The shoals were churned with bursting shells. I saw wounded men among the dead, pined down by the weight of their equipment.

'The first I came to was little Sapper Mullen, the artist. He was submerged to his chin and quite helpless. Somehow I got my scissors out and with my numb hands, which felt weak and useless, I began to cut away his rucksack...

'The Commando were up at the wire and clearly having trouble getting through. I went back to the wounded in the water. I noticed how fast the tide was rising, and wounded men began to shout and scream as they saw they must soon drown. We worked desperately; I don't know how many we pulled clear, though it wasn't more than two or three.'

In one of the vulnerable LCIs (509) carrying the men from No.3

Commando, it was found in an after the battle study that fifty-four out of sixty-three commandos had been killed on the run-in by enemy fire and the inevitable secondary explosions caused by ammunition and fuel. This was no 'cakewalk'.

Yet by mid-morning the accurate German shelling and mortaring of Sword beach had been dramatically reduced. The beach commanders had realized that in the absence of their forward observers (now dead, prisoners or in flight to the rear) the German artillery was ranging on the barrage balloons flying over the area to provide cover against low-flying air attacks. When these had been cut adrift or lowered, the intensity and accuracy of the German gunnery declined. Following the battle a detailed technical analysis showed that the most effective weapon against the assault battalions was the ubiquitous 81 mm mortar much favoured by the Wehrmacht. With an effective range of 2,500 meters it inflicted 6.5% casualties for every 5.7 bombs fired.

The commandos supported by armoured engineers and gun tanks continued their drive into the town and by midday German resistance had spluttered out. Ouistreham was liberated and Frenchmen had played an important role. The population was overwhelmed; Kieffer recalled hearing a young French boy say how delighted he was that the English had been so thoughtful as to bring along soldiers who spoke French.

With Kieffer and the Commandos securing the beach front at Ouistreham and Riva Bella in the east, 8 Infantry Brigade were now pressing south to the Periers ridge leaving a dangerous gap between Sword and Juno sectors and with the follow up waves of 185 and 9 Brigades coming ashore into the now crowded and battle scarred beachhead amongst them was Harry Jones and his platoon from the KSLI. Having escaped from the fire soaked sands on the beach he lead his platoon inland:

'We passed through the village of La Breche and after an advance of about a mile, were soon in the town of Hermanville. As we marched in single file, with a gap of five yards between each man, French people came out doors to welcome us, some shouting "Vive les Anglais", to which I replied in my best Churchillian French "C'est la Liberation". One sight I will never forget was that of the town's chief fireman in full regalia, wearing his large bright brass helmet, rushing down the road to give me a great big hug!

CHAPTER FIVE

HILLMAN AND PERIERS RIDGE
Stands B and C

Route to strongpoint Hillman via Hermanville

Rejoin your transportation and get back on the **D514** by driving from the AVRE passed the memorial square by the hotel and out to the junction with the main road. **Turn left** and **right at the traffic lights** following signs to Hermanville sur Mer on **D60**. This was the road taken by much of 3rd Division as the troops and vehicles pushed inland avoiding flooded lower ground to the east. Before going directly to Hillman it is worth pausing in Hermanville. On entering the village you will note on the left a sign guiding you to the Commonwealth Wargraves Commission. Follow the sign and visit this beautiful cemetery located in Place des Combattants 6 Juin 1944. There are 1,005 burials many being from the 6 June. The burials include 986 British, 13 Canadian, 3 Australian, and 3 French. The British graves include a pair of brothers: the Davis brothers in Plot II Row O graves 7 and 10.

Rejoin the main road into Hermanville and stop in the small square opposite the church. Note the plaque on the wall that describes the use of the Mare Saint Pierre Well by the British Army. Records show that 1,500,000 gallons of potable water were drawn from here between 6 June and 1 July 1944.

Walk up to the Mairie located on the right hand side with its small park and note the plaque on the main gated entrance closest to the Chateau. This plaque recalls that on D-Day 3rd Division established its headquarters here. The

Hermanville-sur-Mer Church and war memorial.

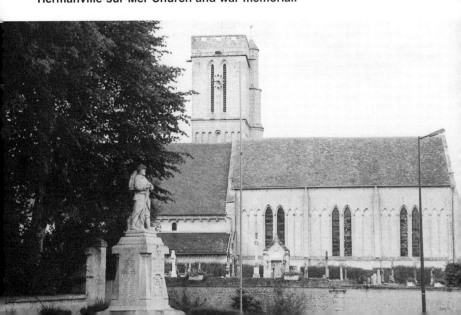

CWGC at Hermanville.

Hermanville Mairie, HQ of 3rd Division on D Day.

Montgomery memorial, Colleville Montgomery.

building and grounds were subsequently used as an important British military hospital.

Across the road in front of the newer Salle Polyvalente is a green plaque and sapling oak tree planted to commemorate Harold Pickersgill MBE who died in 1998. A Citizen of Honour in Hermanville, Harold served in 3rd Reconnaissance Regiment on D-Day, having spent the previous year working on the mapping of German defences in Normandy.

Rejoin your vehicle and proceed **south on the D60** to the junction with the D35. **Turn left** towards Colleville Montgomery. After the water tower on the left and as you enter the village take the **right fork** towards St Aubin d'Arquenay. In Colleville at the crossroads with Rue du Suffolk Regiment look out for the **signpost to Hillman** and **turn right** (south) towards Caen. As you exit the built-up area the road rises and enters a cutting before opening out at the car park and the Hillman fortification. **Park** in the car park and examine the memorial plaque on the first bunker, the NTL post, and the viewpoint on top of the bunker adjacent to the flagpole. Note the schematic map of the position displayed as an orientation table on the concrete plinth. Note also the commemorative plaque on the bunker wall. This reads in English and French:

Hillman bunker and Memorial.

In 1944 this bunker formed part of the strongpoint known as HILLMAN, covering an area 600x400 meters. Hillman consisted of 12 emplacements, with concrete up to 3.5 meters thick. It was armed with anti-tank and machine guns, some in armoured cupolas immune to all tank guns. It was the Regimental HQ for the coast defences of the area, garrisoned by over 150 men. Despite the absence of the planned heavy

123

Looking south from Hillman towards Caen. The farm was defended by the Germans.

The forward bunker of Hillman. A German range card can still be seen on the wall in the right hand weapon pit.

air bombing and naval gun support the position was taken by the 1st Battalion The Suffolk Regiment on 6h June 1944. With the support of C Squadron 13/18th Royal Hussars (QMO), A Sqn Staffordshire Yeomanry, 2 batteries of 33 and 76 Field Regiments Royal Artillery, a detachment of 246 Field Coy Royal Engineers and a machine gun platoon of 2nd Bn The Middlesex Regiment.

Now walk from the car park **using the path** (not the road) to the north towards the seaward edge of the position beyond the hedge. Identify the symbolic cupola and walk over to the well-excavated bunker and stand looking out towards the coast. Note the Tobrouk (open weapon pit) and get in and examine the inner wall and see the very exact German range card painted on its inner side. You are now at grid 957606.

You are facing due north towards Sword Beach which is four kilometres away. You are standing on one of the forward bunkers of strongpoint Hillman. This position was the HQ of the 736th Coastal Defence Regiment, not simply a battalion HQ as the British Army Group, Corps and Divisional intelligence assessments had stated. Hillman extended over a 600x400 metre area and was surrounded by two thick barbed wire fences enclosing a forty foot wide mixed anti-tank and anti-personnel minefield. The thirteen reinforced concrete bunkers, four open weapon pits, and the command post were all inter-connected by trenches. A garrison of 150 personnel manned this fortress. Although essentially on a forward slope (and thus vulnerable to observed long range naval gunfire) it was well sited with excellent fields of fire and observation in almost all directions.

From this second line position you can see the coastline and working from left to right the villages of Luc sur Mer, Lion sur Mer, la Breche where you have just come from, Colleville Plage, Riva Bella and Ouistreham (note the ferry port). On your right from Riva Bella running South-South West to Caen is the River Orne and its canal. Three kilometers southeast from here lies Benouville and Pegasus Bridge, seized just after midnight by Major John Howard and his gliderborne company. To your right rear and beyond the Orne, lies the Colombelles steelworks, much reduced in size now but still in evidence. In 1944 its original chimney-stacks and buildings provided cover to German observation posts and troops from 21st Panzer Division. To your immediate rear beyond the hedge line, lies the memorial bunker dedicated to the men of the Suffolk Regiment who captured Hillman on D-Day. Eight kilometers to your rear lies Caen itself – the divisional objective on D-Day.

German range indicators are still in evidence in this Hillman bunker.

Queen Beach: Engineers and No.5 Beach Group work to improve a lane leading off the foreshore.

Navy and Army personnel of the Beach Group on Sword Beach.

The Move Inland

The reader can now follow the story of 3rd Division's thrust inland and specifically the actions of the 1st Battalion the Suffolk Regiment. This was the reserve battalion of 8 Infantry Brigade. Having landed, the Suffolk rifle companies had moved off the congested beach to the west in order to find a suitable exit. The Commanding Officer (CO) met the second-in-command of the South Lancashires who informed him that his CO had been 'badly hit' on the beach (he was in fact killed in action). Having found the prepared exits off the two now very crowded beach subsectors, the companies moved to their assembly area about 800 meters inland. Bullets and shells were flying about in all directions but few casualties were taken. Unfortunately, and most seriously for the day's subsequent operations, Captain Llewellyn RA, the Forward Observer Bombardment (FOB), and his party were hit by a mortar bomb as they left their LCA. They had all been killed or wounded.

Without the FOB it would not now be possible to call on the fire support from the dedicated cruiser and destroyer for the subsequent battalion attack on strongpoint Hillman.

The assembly area on arrival was found to be devoid of cover. The trees, which had been there on a recent air photo, had all been cut down probably to make 'Rommel's asparagus.' A German rifleman was hidden amongst the remaining piles of brushwood, but he was either quickly killed or made-off after the battalion arrived in force. The CO now decided to move two or three hundred metres further inland to an orchard where the companies could assemble in some cover. On arrival at his new location, an officer and five other ranks of a Canadian parachute unit who had been dropped in the wrong place during the night emerged and greeted them. They had spent an uncomfortable early morning, having been bombed by Allied planes and shelled by the fleet. They were glad to see the battalion and despite their experiences were determined to get on with the battle. They joined D Company for the morning.

At this stage large packs were taken off and breaching platoons from D Company joined A and B Companies. During this time, the enemy caused little trouble to the battalion although they did start mortaring the area of the cut down wood that had only just been abandoned. Off to the east a multi-barrelled mortar was firing towards the beach. Suddenly a ship started firing salvo after salvo for some ten

British infantry moving off Sword Beach.

minutes into a field about 100 metres to the east of the CO's orders group. The Liaison Officer (LO) Captain Wardlaw from C Squadron 13/18th Hussars reported in his tank to say that the squadron had got safely ashore and was on its way to join the battalion. They were now ready to move, but there was still no sign of Rear Battalion HQ with the second in command and adjutant. They had in fact traveled in a LCI, which had been hit forward as it approached the beach and both landing ramps had been put out of action. The LCI had to pull-off and those aboard were transferred to other landing craft. They finally turned up about an hour late.

It was from this forward Assembly Area that Captain Elliott commanding the antitank platoon was sent on a lonely mission to make contact with the 6th Airborne Division astride the Orne. He successfully completed this dangerous task covering some Fourteen kilometres that day, which he later described as rather like 'walking across the front of the [range] butts at Bisley during a rapid fire practice'.

In his Assembly Area, the CO confirmed his orders and the companies moved off according to plan. D Company, less the two breaching platoons, moved south to a position where they could observe and bring fire down upon Strongpoint Morris that was their immediate objective. They found mine fields marked with boards showing the skull and crossbones and the words 'Achtung Minen', but the mines did not form a continuous obstacle and thus did not hinder their progress. C Company moved off immediately after, with a troop of tanks southeastwards towards Colleville followed by the remainder of the battalion. [Those left out of battle (LOB) remained behind under Captain Coppock; Major Gordon, who should have been in command of this group, had not yet turned-up being in the damaged LCI with Rear Battalion HQ.]

On the move to the village, the route chosen was through orchards where cattle were still grazing, this implied that there were no mines. Not long after the troops had left the assembly area a multi-barrelled mortar opened up on it. The bombs could be seen quite easily, and made an uncanny wailing noise. Luckily there were no casualties among the LOB. It was also noted that several of the bombs were duds and failed to explode.

In Colleville some of the commandos from 1st Special Service Brigade, who had landed twenty minutes after the battalion were encountered. They were from No.6 Commando and had just cleared two pillboxes north of Colleville. They had two or three frightened

Men of the 1st Suffolks moving inland on the morning of D-Day.

looking prisoners who were interrogated but produced little information of any value; one prisoner was a Pole. The commandos said they wanted to go and deal with the multi-barrelled mortar. They were given a couple of the 13th/18th tanks by the battalion and they moved off to do the settling. The mortar crew, wisely, quickly withdrew. The time would have been about 1030 hours. Also at about this time, the CO of 1 Suffolk met Lord Lovat the commander of 1st Special Service Brigade at the northern end of Colleville. He was described as looking as if he were out for a country walk. Colonel (then Major) Gough writing in 1991 related how he watched Lovat, at the head of his commandos marching in threes as if on a route march lead by Bill Millin with his bagpipes. They left for the Orne bridges by way of St Aubin d'Arquenay (to the northeast). After clearing scattered opposition on the way they got to the bridges at about 1330 hours.

The Clearing of Colleville

Meanwhile C Company had started to clear of the village assisted by a troop of C Squadron 13/18th Hussars. In 1944 Colleville stretched for well over a kilometre along its main road, with two parallel roads or tracks on each side. There were probably nearly a hundred separate buildings in all. The issued maps showed some fieldworks in the area of the village with some motor transport bays marked near the church at the north end with more field works and wire at the southeast corner. Otherwise there was no information about whether it was defended. It is now known that the Germans did occupy houses in the village; one was a mess for the officers of Hillman and one was the headquarters mess for the artillery unit at Point 61; in addition to the individual German billets in various private houses.

C Company, under Major Boycott, quickly completed its mission of ensuring that the village was secured. They found few Germans and therefore had little problem as they worked through the village. In fact they had missed a couple of the enemy who had gone into hiding, and the next day some shots were fired by them from the church tower. By this time there were a great number of different British units around the northern end of the village. There was an immediate response from the gunners and tanks in the vicinity. One tank gun put a 75mm round through the tower and two Germans covered with dust gave themselves up shortly afterwards.

Corporal Ashby of C Company described how as part of the point section he went along the street of the village past the church to the Mairie. There his section established a defensive position on the first floor overlooking the street. Shortly after, Monsieur le Maire emerged from his shelter and joined them. So at 1000 hours on the morning D-Day he found himself sharing a bottle of Calvados and information concerning German dispositions with Monsieur Lenauld the mayor of Colleville.

In the meantime, Major Papillion, who was to die at Chateau de la Londe a month later, had reported from his position with C Company that the support squadron of the 13/18th was now in position off to his west and exchanging shots with Hillman. He also reported that there appeared to be no movement from Morris.

Morris was a four-gun 105-mm battery, three guns being housed in two-metre thick concrete emplacement; the fourth was still under construction on D-Day. Two belts of barbed wire further protected the bunkers. The outer wire obstacle was nine feet wide and the inner fence was three feet deep. In between was a mixed minefield (anti-tank and

Aerial photograph taken a week before D-Day showing the two strongpoints code-named 'Morris' and 'Hillman' by the Allies. White dots are anti-glider poles. Morris gave up without a fight; Hillman put up strong resistance.

anti-personnel). Six machine guns and an ant-aircraft gun covered these perimeter defenses. As C Company was meeting no effective opposition in clearing the village the CO sent for Major McCaffrey commanding B Company and told him that it was possible that the enemy had already deserted the battery position. However, he was ordered to prepare his attack as arranged just in case it was a ruse. Major McCaffrey ordered his company quickly up into the village behind C Company. As soon as he had 'elbow room' he moved towards this formidable battery position for the attack.

As B Company started preparing for its assault on Morris the guns of the supporting battery started to register on the target area. In view of the lack of fight shown so far, McCaffrey decided to quicken the procedure by blowing the outer wire before calling for an artillery concentration. However, just as the Bangalore torpedoes were being placed, a white flag was put up and the entire garrison emerged from their concrete emplacements with their hands up. There were sixty-seven Germans in all. They were brought back into the village by four highly delighted soldiers who moved them along the main street at the point of their bayonets at a smart pace. The garrison was not in good shape. They had suffered some heavy air raids on the 1st and 2nd of June, one of which is now known to have caused many casualties.

The Germans occupying Morris gave up without a fight. Here a British Tommy hangs out his washing at the rear entrance of the casemate to the west of the defence complex.

That morning Morris was allegedly attacked by the USAAF although there had not been any direct hits. The navy had then started a bombardment with the 6-inch guns from HMS *Dragon* and the guns of the destroyer *Kelvin*. A naval air spotter should have controlled their fire but they reported that they had difficulties in communicating with the aircraft. *Dragon* therefore was unable to engage Morris except by blind, estimated fire. Once the position was occupied it was discovered that the guns were still fully serviceable; a photograph taken a fortnight later showed one of the guns apparently intact, except for a small jagged hole in the gun shield, presumably from a shell or bomb splinter. The positions can still be seen today integrated into newer houses and gardens on the western outskirts of Colleville to the south of the D35a. They are still in very much the state they were left in in 1944, with no apparent damage from all the explosives hurled at them. The psychological effect of that bombardment, however, was enough for the battery troops to give up without a fight.

By midday the battalion was able to report that Morris had been cleared. Ten minutes after B Company confirmed that there was no enemy left in Morris the position was engaged by guns firing from the southeast (perhaps from the German battery just north of Periers sur le Dan or from the self propelled 150-mm battery of 17/16 regiment at Plumetot). Fortunately there were no casualties. The men from B Company were either sheltering in the concrete defences they had just taken, or were well outside the position. B Company now moved up to take supporting positions for A Company's forthcoming attack on Hillman.

The First Attack on Hillman

As the enemy adjusted their shelling of Morris towards the south of the village, A Company was using a route to the east of the village away from the enemy bunkers so as to get into a suitable position from which to attack Hillman. Unfortunately they suffered some casualties from this blind shelling. One section of 9 Platoon was nearly wiped out with seven casualties from one shell, including a regimental signaler who was killed.

About a hundred metres clear of the village a Canadian parachute officer met up with the CO. He had been dropped in the wrong place and was accompanied by a sergeant who had broken his arm during the night-drop; the NCO received treatment at the Regimental Aid Post while the officer took the CO to a position from which Hillman could be overlooked; peering through the standing corn – then some 18-

Geschützunterstellraum II

M 1:150

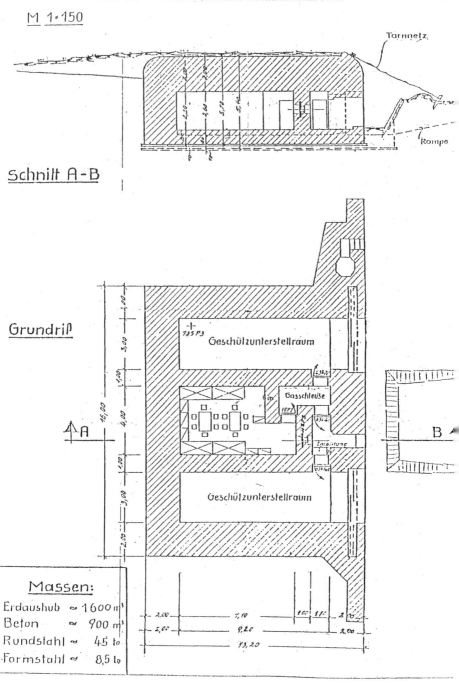

Schnitt A-B

Grundriß

Geschützunterstellraum

Gasschleuse

Geschützunterstellraum

Tarnnetz

Rampe

Massen:

Erdaushub ≈ 1600 m³
Beton ≈ 900 m³
Rundstahl ≈ 45 to
Formstahl ≈ 8,5 to

German Todt Organization bunker plan.

inches high – it was possible to see the outer wire some 150 metres away. It was difficult to see much more detail because of the corn, but one steel cupola was visible. Meanwhile C Company sent one platoon forward to provide flank protection to A Company and another platoon was directed through the orchards on the outskirts of Colleville so that they could cover across the open country. By doing this C Company had quickly established a flank security position for the next stage of the overall battalion plan.

D Company with a breaching platoon from B Company now waited in reserve at the southern end of the village. So at this stage, the tactical dispositions were:

A Company: reinforced waiting to attack.

B Company: on the right prepared to support the assault company.

C Company: left forward.

D Company: close by in the village to provide mutual support.

Major 'Jock' Waring, the battery commander from 76th Field Regiment was in the meantime registering his guns on the position. The Battalion's own 3-inch mortars had also moved up into position and were also ranging-in on the fortress. There were, however, some difficulties with the artillery registration. This was because the No.18 Radio Set, which was the only means of communication between Major Waring and his gun line, was not working well. Many problems emerged on D-Day because of the inferior communications on the smaller radio sets. Many of the communications difficulties were certainly caused by the very great density of radios working in a very confined area. It may also have been hampered because the radios had been 'netted' several days prior to embarkation; as a result some sets had almost certainly come 'off-net'.

At about 1130 hours Captain Ryley set off on his own reconnaissance of Hillman. Although he can have had few illusions about the task to be done he must have begun to realize just how difficult his mission really was on seeing the extent of this fortress. His reconnaissance indicated that there had been no effective preparatory bombing of the position although there were some bomb craters close to the wire; fifty-three years on it seems that the poor weather on D-Day had prevented the USAAF from completing this priority-bombing mission in the early hours of the morning of 6 June. Tragically, as a result of the loss of the FOB Party, he was now also deprived of the use of the available naval guns on HMS *Dragon*. He was also rather surprised to see the armoured cupolas in the position of which he had received no warning.

Oberst Krug.

From the excellent vantage point at Hillman the German garrison could observe the invasion fleet and the progress of British troops as they made their way inland towards them.

Inside the fortress *Oberst* Krug, the commanding officer of 736th Regiment, had been alerted very early in the morning that something out of the ordinary was going on. At 0140 hours he had told his divisional commander about the nearby airborne landings. Throughout the small hours of the morning he would have been aware of the attempts by 21st Panzer Division to retake the bridges at Benouville, and heard the tank exploding in the village near the canal in the failed attempt to push Howard's men off the Orne bridges. At first light he and his men would have looked north and seen the great armada out to sea and have witnessed the assault on the beaches and its deadly progress inland. There could have been few surprises for the garrison at Hillman that morning with their grandstand view of D-Day. Even though 7th Army and Army Group B both considered the overall situation to be under control at 0530 hours there could have been few tactical commanders in this area that felt quite so optimistic as daybreak illuminated the terrible spectacle.

By 1300 hours, Captain Ryley of the Suffolk's had notified his CO that he was ready to attack Hillman. 'Grab', the codeword for the supporting fire mission was sent over the airwaves at 1310 hours by the CO. At that time the guns began their five minutes of shelling together with the tanks of C Squadron, and the battalion's 3-inch mortars. The men of D Company's breaching platoon now crept forward to the outer wire to carry out their allotted task. This approach was to be followed by A Company, by way of a sunken path (not apparent on the air photos and may

Route of 1
Suffolks fro
Colleville

Hillman.

actually have been the road to Hillman itself) to within a fairly short
distance of the wire. Thereafter they were able to crawl through the
corn to the outer wire. They were protected from sight to some extent
because of the undergrowth that had been allowed to flourish around
the position.

Platoons of A Company were deployed on either side to provide
additional protection for the breaching party. The bangalore torpedoes
were pushed under the twelve feet of outer wire and blown. The mine
clearance party, with sapper help, then started on the clearing of a
three-foot wide lane through the minefield that they marked with
white tape. When the inner wire was reached the second Bangalore
section came up and placed the torpedoes under the wire. The platoon
commander was then placed in a tricky position as the initiating device
of the Bangalore failed to go off. He then had to go through the
minefield to obtain another one and this time he was successful. His
platoon carried out its task very effectively, working as if on a training
exercise, yet within only fifty metres of an alert enemy. The
commander's bravery and leadership was subsequently recognised by

the award of the Croix de Guerre.

Unfortunately, the use of phosphorous grenades thrown by the zealous covering party to hide the breaching team's movement, served only to draw the attention of the Germans onto their activities. Once the machine gun in the cupola, only thirty metres away, had located the breach any activity in the area drew a lethal hail of bullets.

The first assault platoon moved forward through the breach crawling all the way from the narrow sunken lane. The platoon did get through the gap but they then came under heavy machine-gun fire and a section commander was killed. Lieutenant Powell, the platoon commander, then came forward with a PIAT team. Three shots were fired at the cupola, which was causing most of the trouble. These had no evident effect. The rest of the platoon had now advanced into the trenches in the position but this did little good as the enemy merely withdrew into their concrete shelters and opened fire with machine guns from behind armoured doors at any attempt to move against them. A message was sent back to say the platoon was held up but the runner was killed on the way back and a second runner had to be sent.

Under cover of a further concentration of fire (HE and smoke) the second platoon went in, this time led by the company commander. Once again machine-gun fire opened up and only four men managed to get through the gap in the wire. Alone, they went forward for over 150 metres and took a few prisoners. As they were unable to continue without reinforcements, Lieutenant Powell went back while the others waited for assistance. He returned with three men but found that Lieutenant Tooley and Corporal Stares had both been badly wounded (and later died). Captain Ryley was killed shortly afterwards when returning for more support. Other wounded from the vicinity of the gap were now being dragged back through the corn to the sunken lane from where stretcher-bearers carried them back to the now busy Regimental Aid Post in Colleville. Throughout this period Lieutenant Powell displayed great leadership and courage. He was rightly awarded the MC but was killed at Tinchebray in southern Normandy shortly after the award was announced.

The Second Attack on Hillman

By this time the CO's carrier and the battery commander's tank had at last escaped from the traffic jam on the beach. This gave the CO a radio link with the tank squadron through the N0.19 set in the carrier and also provided the battery commander with effective communications to his guns. Before that, communications had been

Steel cupola with machine guns and periscope.

possible to the squadron through the LO's tank but the CO's carrier was now able to come right up to a forward position whereas his tank could not come forward without being seen.

As there appeared to be no antitank guns left in action in the position the CO ordered the tanks up to the outer wire in order to give the troops close support. This move did not materially improve the situation as the 75-mm guns were unable to penetrate the emplacements and the enemy was still able to prevent any movement through the breach and into the perimeter by unprotected infantry. Even 17-pounder armour piercing shot only gouged the metal and could not penetrate the steel cupola that was causing most of the trouble. The situation was a stalemate and the CO appreciated that it would not be possible to capture this fortress position without great loss unless the tanks went through the wire, thus enabling the infantry to move up with the tanks up to the emplacements and so destroy or capture the enemy at close quarters. He decided to have a vehicle gap made and to lay on a fresh attack with a repeat bombardment. Colonel Alan Sperling's recollection of these events was dominated by the calmness of the CO's planning and orders while under continuous fire.

Yet there was certainly one, perhaps two, antitank guns still in action on Hillman; one tank was hit without damage when firing on the position from the north but when 4 Troop of C Squadron moved off to the east in the open country between Hillman and St Aubin d'Arquenay two tanks were hit resulting in casualties in both vehicles; later in the afternoon one tank was completely knocked out by Hillman's 75mm gun. The FOO's tank from 7 Field Regiment supporting the Norfolks was also hit but only lost its radio; meanwhile in one of the myriad small actions which make up momentous battles, 4 Troop had the satisfaction of 'shooting up' an antitank gun in the open, catching its crew turning the gun around to take them on!

The CO then ordered Lieutenant Perry, who had now taken over command of A Company, to withdraw his men from the position so as to get them clear for a repeat bombardment and to rest them in the sunken lane. He sent for his attached RE officer, Lieutenant Arthur Heal, and told him the gap had to be widened to nine feet. Heal told the CO that the quickest way to do this was to use flails. He then came up to reconnoiter the position. He and Cpl Boulton and a sapper from his detachment crawled flat on their bellies to find out more about the minefield. It was initially thought that it might have been a dummy one. However, Heal found a mine and started carefully examining it. He had made himself familiar with all types of German mines likely to be found, but here was one that he did not recognise. With some trepidation he pulled it out and studied it more closely: he was relieved to find it was an obsolete British Mk III mine probably captured at Dunkirk. He also discovered that the mines were in four rows at about five metre intervals.

He returned to the CO to report his findings. He was asked how long it would take to make a proper gap. Heal said about an hour but suggested he could do a quicker job using gelignite charges to blow a row of mines providing a gap of about five yards. The tank commander was agreeable to this, so he set off once again with his Lance Corporal working flat on the ground under fire to clear sufficient mines for a tank gap. A rifle platoon and one of the tanks provided covering fire.

Lieutenant Colonel Nigel Tapp (now Major General Sir Nigel Tapp), who was then commanding 7th Field Regiment in support of 185 Brigade, graphically described the local situation at this time. He arrived at Colleville at about 1400 hours to find a scene of great confusion. He recalls seeing two tanks, which had advanced up to the track to Hillman, had been blown up on mines thus blocking the track. There were dead men and burning motorcycles in the street. The Norfolks, part of 185 Brigade, were close behind them and more tanks and vehicles of the 8 Brigade group were blocking the roads leading to the village. Major Dunn, the battery commander with 1 Norfolk, has also described how the FOO from 76th Field Regiment had gone off in his tank thinking that he would deal with a German machine gun post holding up A Company. Shortly afterwards there was a loud explosion and he came back to say his tank had gone up on a mine. Colonel Dick Goodwin has also related this story but added that the squadron LO went off with the battery commander and that it was his tank that went up. The CO described the tank as being a complete writeoff, one track being blown off and the tank burnt out; the LO came back to say he had 'a slight headache.'

Colonel Dick Goodwin.

The divisional commander, Tom Rennie, now came up to the CO's observation post and asked how the battalion was getting on. When he was told the situation he said:

> *'well you must get it before dark; and in time to allow you to dig in on your consolidated positions. Enemy armour is about and they will probably counter-attack at first light.'*

The CO assured him that 1 Suffolk would succeed. He left with a cheery 'Good luck'. General Rennie would be wounded a few days later driving over a mine and then killed at the Rhine crossing commanding 51st Highland Division the following year.

Shortly afterwards the brigade commander (Brigadier E E E Cass) arrived. The CO asked him for two flails to speed up the process of mine clearance and for further tank support. He agreed to do this and soon afterwards the CO was informed on the radio that two flails were coming up. A Squadron, Staffordshire Yeomanry, were in reserve not far away and they were ordered to come forward and assist. The flails eventually turned up well after a sufficient gap had been cleared to let the tanks enter the position. The squadron commander was just starting to report to Lieutenant Colonel Dick Goodwin when he received urgent orders to redeploy and meet a threatened tank attack by 21st Panzer Division. The squadron rapidly moved off and subsequently knocked out three enemy tanks from positions to the west of Bieville.

While all this was going on, the Norfolks had tried to bypass Hillman in two groups. Two companies led by the second in command followed the line of a track leading southwest from Colleville. They had strict orders not to become involved in the Hillman battle. Their information was that the village of St Aubin d'Arquenay, cleared by the commandos earlier, was still held by the enemy. This was to prove a disaster because the battalion now selected a route that took them across the cornfields between St Aubin and the eastern bunkers at Hillman. Both the leading and the following companies (A and B respectively) got involved in a firefight and both suffered many casualties; in all they probably had over forty killed and wounded – including A Company commander – as they were drawn into a battle that they had no reason to be involved in. Eyewitness accounts state that some casualties were caused by friendly fire from British supporting tanks. Too late the Norfolks had learned that St Aubin was already clear.

By this time it was mid-afternoon (the Staffordshire Yeomanry tanks were recalled at 1615 hours). Arthur Heal and his sappers had, by now, cleared a gap through the minefield sufficiently wide for tanks. Their excellent work under fire from these active enemy positions (one sapper was wounded) was recognised by the award of the MM to corporal Boulton and the Croix de Guerre to Lieutenant Heal.

The CO now called for a repeat bombardment of five minutes HE from the artillery. When this lifted the tanks started to go through the gap. The leading tank however refused to drive over the British dead body still obstructing the path ahead. Corporal Lawson, the section commander, had no intention of losing any more lives and told the tank commander in no uncertain terms to 'fing well proceed'. The troops followed the tank through the gap and fanned out in either direction using cover from shell holes beyond the perimeter wire. Tank main armament had still proven incapable of penetrating the cupola from which machine gun fire continued to be directed at any dismounted personnel.

Corporal Lawson and Private 'Tich' Hunter of 8 Platoon found themselves within twenty metres of the cupola. Suddenly one lone German came running towards them hands raised in surrender. A shot rang out and he was killed. The tension had been too much for one British soldier. Soon afterwards Hunter stood up from his shelter in a bomb hole and slowly and determinedly walked towards the cupola firing his Bren gun from the hip. This had the desired effect as no further resistance came form this direction and the mopping up began. Hunter was awarded the DCM for his bravery. The network of trenches was by now deserted except for one dead German. Hunter jumped down and was looking at the body when Corporal Lawson glancing to

'Tich' Hunter.

the right, saw a lone German, rifle raised. Lawson shouted a warning and the bullet just grazed Hunter's forehead. The German disappeared round the corner of the trench that led into one of the concreted emplacements. Grenades were dropped down the ventilation shafts that had some effect as their occupants started to come out with hands up in surrender.

The companies then carried out the moppingup with the support of the tanks. Some of these tanks raced ahead alone and had to be recalled. The process was a long and tedious one as the Germans were safely ensconced in their concrete and steel and the area was a large one. The pioneers were called in to use their beehive charges to blow in some of the emplacements. Eventually all firing ceased at about 2000 hours and the position was secured with no further apparent resistance. In addition to the casualties inflicted on the garrison some fifty prisoners were taken.

The CO had ordered B and D Companies forward to their consolidation areas as soon as he saw that the position was nearing capture. A and C Companies followed, so that the whole battalion was firmly in position and dugin facing Caen just before dark. The mortar platoon and antitank platoon had also been hastily dug in, the antitank platoon suffering one casualty in the process. A gun being towed by a carrier was to be sited at the far corner of the enemy position, but as it was going through the gap in the minefield through which a squadron of tanks had passed without any difficulty, the carrier was blown up by a mine. The carrier and gun were destroyed but there were only minor injuries to the two men in the front of the carrier, the remainder of the crew being on foot.

The squadron from the 13th/18th also withdrew about 1930 hours to rally near battalion HQ where they were able to replenish their ammunition stocks. Apart from the losses to tanks to enemy action, the squadron commander, much to his great annoyance, had the misfortune to lose his tank when it fell into the officers latrine on Hillman where it broke a track. The tanks were later to take up positions below the Periers ridge to counter the threat from 21st Panzer Division. Just after the troops had left Hillman the enemy opened up with artillery and mortars but the shells fell beyond battalion HQ except for one mortar bomb that hit the office truck, setting it on fire and causing three casualties.

Beauvais farm (on the ridge directly to the south of Hillman) was in D Company's consolidation area. As the leading troops approached it, two enemy riflemen were found in the corn and dispatched. The CSM then said that he could see movement through a window in the farm, about 250 metres away. He fired a round and saw someone fall down. 17 Platoon was given the task of clearing the buildings. They approached via a line of trees but they then had about a hundred metres of open space to cross. No sign of life was to be seen; the Bren guns were positioned to cover the farm from the right flank and the platoon prepared to assault. With a burst from the Brens the platoon was off but they immediately saw on the left, troops climbing out of slit trenches with their hands in the air shouting 'kamerad'; all surrendered, two officers and forty-eight men in total. They left behind four machine guns and their rifles together with a great many stick grenades. Their packs and parcels were all laid out in threes ready for surrender – by the time the farm was reached. The company commander (Major Papillon) now decided to stand back about 250 metre's from the farm to dig-in for the night. This was a wise decision as the enemy positions were later mortared, on and off for about an hour with no casualties to D Company.

It was at that stage of consolidation that the Air-Landing Brigade of 6th Airborne Division had appeared overhead. This was a magnificent and heart-warming sight as the enormous flight of Dakotas towing their gliders flew over in perfect formation to land away beyond St. Aubin d'Arquenay. They were followed by a large number of Stirlings dropping coloured parachutes with containers of equipment. One can imagine the dramatic effect that this display of Allied air power gave to the recently bloodied assault troops and the correspondingly depressing effect it must have had on the Germans struggling to reestablish control of a rapidly deteriorating situation.

The battalion stood to that evening from 2230 to 2330 hours and then started patrolling. It had been a long and eventful day. For many it had started at 0330 hours that morning and had included an uncomfortable trip through rough seas in un-seaworthy landing craft. It had ended with all the battalion objectives taken at the cost of seven killed and twenty-five wounded. About 200 prisoners had been taken in addition to the battle casualties inflicted on the enemy. Other losses included one man who died of his wounds and seven others who were less severely wounded from C Squadron 13th/18th Hussars. The detachment from 246 Company RE had one man wounded and the

A dramatic display of Allied air power was demonstrated on the afternoon of D-Day when the Air-Landing Brigade of the 6th Airborne Division appeared over the battlefield to reinforce the air landings east of the Orne.

Note 3rd Division Tactical sign for an anti-tank battery location.

Umgehu
Caen - No

platoon of 2nd Middlesex had one man killed and six wounded in Colleville by a mortar bomb.

On the face of it, all was quiet on Hillman. The battalion occupied positions all around and over it. But there was still some activity inside the main bunker network. General Richter, commander of 716th Division writing in a report dated 23 June 1944, stated that the resistance nest at Point 61 (confused for Hillman itself) had successfully defended itself and remained in unbroken communications with his divisional HQ.

SS-S*tandartenführer* **Hubert Meyer.**

An extraordinary incident took place at midnight, 6 June, that is worth recounting; at about that time *Standartenführer* Hubert Meyer of 12th SS Panzer Division walked into Richter's underground HQ just outside Caen. Richter told Meyer that he had no news. None of his positions were now reporting. No dispatch riders had been able to get through. The situation was entirely confused. Then the telephone rang. It was *Oberst* Krug, the commander of 736 Grenadier Regiment deep underground in his bunker inside the now overrun Hillman position. He is reported to have said: 'the enemy are on top of my bunker. I have no means of resisting them and no communications with my men. What shall I do?' Richter's helpful reply was: 'I can give you no more orders. You must make your own decision now. Goodbye.'

At 0645 hours next morning, Oberst Krug immaculately turned out in his highly polished boots, came out of his underground HQ with his batman and two packed suitcases; three other officers and seventy other ranks then surrendered with him. The prisoners were searched before they were escorted to the beach. The second in command took a briefcase containing maps and documents from Krug, which was then passed back to battalion HQ. The place where the surrendering party emerged was close to the bunker on which the memorial to those who fell on D-Day is erected. Also close-by was a hut containing a great cache of champagne and Vichy water Krug was clearly a man of taste! Other accounts of Oberst Krug refer to much 'heel clicking' going on in the village as he said farewell to his men before they moved on. Many in his command had viewed him as an Austrian of the 'old school' and very 'sensible'.

Stand C – Periers Ridge and the German Counter Attack

Route to Stand C

From Hillman retrace your route to the centre of Colleville and **turn west** on **D35**. After a short distance (one block) turn **left** on the **D60a** towards Periers-sur-le-Dan. Look to you left as you leave the village and note Hillman's dominating position on the skyline. At the main crossroads (formerly known as Point 61) go **straight on** along the D220 to the outskirts of Periers and take the **right turn** at the crossroads on the D222 go up the hill; at the top of the crest (Periers Ridge) stop at Point 55 where the **farm track crosses the road**.

Orientation

You are now at Point 55 on D222 between Plumetot and Periers-sur-le-Dan at Grid 929611 on a track and road junction facing southwest. You are located about 4,000 metres from Stand A at La Breche d'Hermanville. Caen is nine kilometres further south of the Periers Ridge. Look to the northwest and identify Plumetot. Look southwest and identify Mathieu. Look southeast and locate Periers-sur-le-Dan, Point 61, and Hillman.

The Drive for Caen on D-Day Falters

While the Suffolk's and 8 Brigade had been fighting their way inland, 185 Brigade had landed and formed up at Hermanville. By 1100 hours it was ready to start its thrust for Caen. The brigade plan had ordered the KSLI to lead, on a general axis from Beauville Lebisey, carried on, and supported by, tanks of the Staffordshire Yeomanry. However, the Yeomanry was still queuing up at the beach exits caught in that mother of all traffic jams. Lieutenant Colonel Maurice commanding the KSLI waited until midday (a 1 hour delay) and was then given permission by his brigade commander, Brigadier KP Smith, to advance on foot. At that moment 7th Field Regiment RA had just got clear of the beach congestion and roared through Hermanville past the KSLI and went into action in the fields south of the village to become the foremost troops on the Divisional axis.

The KSLI started off and before long the Staffordshire Yeomanry caught them up. Near Periers they came upon a German howitzer battery against which a company/squadron attack was mounted. The enemy fought doggedly but eventually a Pole among them was captured who showed Major Wheelock commanding Z Company a route in through the wire at the back of the battery position. The attack went in and by late evening the position was secure. Meanwhile the main body of the KSLI and Staffordshire Yeomanry group had pushed on and secured Bieville by 1600 hours. At about 1615 hours the reconnaissance troop of the Yeomanry then reported that a company of panzers was approaching fast from the direction of Caen. The number of tanks being observed rapidly increased to a total of forty. 21-year-old Lieutenant Harry Jones of the KSLI also witnessed the arrival of the panzers. While standing with his company commander and pouring over a map, a German shell exploded near them:

> *'I looked towards the enemy and could not believe my eyes. There advancing round the corner of a wood about five hundred yards away, were five or six German tanks! We hurriedly dispersed and I returned to my platoon...I could still hear the sound of German tanks firing and was relieved to hear the sound of our own anti-tank guns and those of the Staffordshire Yeomanry tanks.'*

This was the predicted intervention of 21st Panzer Division and specifically the 1st *Abteilung* from 22 Regiment commanded by Hauptmann Von Gottberg. The KSLI and Yeomanry hand rapidly deployed to meet the threat. From Bieville north along the Periers Ridge there was now a hastily but well sited anti-tank screen consisting of a squadron of the Yeomanry together with the KSLI's 6-pounder antitank platoon and a troop of 41st Antitank Battery RA with 17-pounders around Bieville while the Shermans of B Squadron of the Yeomanry were to the north around Periers. In sum a broad and formidable anti-tank screen had been quickly emplaced along the southwestern flank of 3rd Division's beachhead.

The German Counter-Attack

But why had it taken so long for the Germans to respond in any strength to the threat to Caen? After a night of confusion the 22 Panzer Regiment had been ordered to attack 6th Airborne Division. So, at 0900 hours they were struggling back through Caen over the few remaining bridges towards the airborne bridgehead. At 1030 hours 7th Army then ordered the regiment to turn around and attack the beaches: objective Lion-sur-Mer. By this stage the lead battalion was already in contact with 6th Airborne Division. At 1300 hours the divisional commander – Edgar Feuchtinger then ordered the force to split into three *Kampfgruppen* two for west of the Orne and one *Kampfgruppen* under Hans Von Luck committed to recapture the two bridges from the eastern bank. Hans Von Luck recounted to the author how this disorder, regrouping and the constant air attacks took their toll on the force's effectiveness and tempo. The move from the east bank of the Orne was hampered by the loss of the Orne bridges. This forced the columns to move via Colombelles and Caen in order to reach Lebisey Ridge. Refugees impeded their journey along with debris filled streets,

General Edgar Feuchtinger, commander of 21st Panzer Division inspects one of his assault-gun units.

and a further Allied air attack on Caen around 1330 hours. Then as the armoured columns exited the city they were engaged by eight rocket-firing Typhoons that knocked out six tanks.

By the time von Oppeln-Bronikowski had brought his depleted tank regiment — now consisting of three tank battalions (Abteilung I, II and III), the fourth being attached to Von Luck's Panzergrenadier Regiment 125 — to Lebisey Ridge at about 1600 hours he was surprised to find General Marcks, commander of 84th Corps, waiting for him. After further dividing his tank assets between *Kampfgruppe* Rauch (one tank *Abteilung)* and his own *Kampfgruppe* Oppeln (the remaining two *Abteilung)*, the Corps Commander briefed him saying, *'Oppeln, if you don't succeed in throwing the British into the sea we shall have lost the war!'* With the order *'Panzer marsch'* given at 1620 hours they set off in two powerful assault groups:

***Oberst* Hermann von Oppeln-Bronikowski.**

151

Kampfgruppe **Rauch: West**
  2 Armoured infantry battalions
  1 Tank *Abteilung*
  1 Armoured engineers battalion
  1 Artillery Battalion
Kampfgruppe **Oppeln: East**
  2 Tank *Abteilung*
  1 Armoured infantry battalion
  1 Engineer battalion
  1 Artillery (armoured) Battalion

Having negotiated their way around the German anti-tank obstacle sited just to the north of Lebisey, the right hand, eastern, column hit Bieville and the British anti-tank screen head-on; two panzers were knocked out by the Yeomanry and a further two tanks destroyed by the KSLI antitank gunners. The remaining panzers swung to the west pursued by two troops of A Squadron who knocked out four more enemy tanks and a further two fell to the No. 4 gun of 41 Battery. The panzers continued northwest and ran straight into B Squadron who were waiting for them hulldown behind Periers ridge.

An account from 21st Panzer Division's unofficial history states:

> *'The British positions were tactically well chosen and their fire both heavy and accurate. The first mark IV was blazing before a single [German] tank had the chance to fire a shot. The remainder moved forward firing to where the enemy were thought to be; but the English weapons were well concealed and within a few minutes we had lost six tanks, meanwhile, sweeping round to the left of Periers rise, were the thirty-five tanks led by Hauptmann von Gottberg; they attacked point 61 held by a squadron of the Staffordshire. The position was the same. The fire of the English from their outstandingly well-sited defensive positions was murderous.'*

This group was also repulsed losing ten tanks. Within a short space of time, the armoured regiment of 21st Panzer Division had lost a total of sixteen tanks, a decisive moral defeat from which it never really recovered. In an account given in Alexander McKee's *Caen Anvil of Victory* and by Kortenhaus in his privately published history of 21st Panzer Division they state:

> *'The long wait from the early morning in addition to the diversion via Colombelles had consumed fourteen hours and given the enemy time to build up a strong line of defence. The one and only chance on D-Day had been lost. Never again was there to be such an opportunity.'*

While very successful for 3rd Division this brief skirmish had now

Panzer IVs of 22nd Regiment, 21st Panzer Division, moving against the invasion front.

settled the fate of Caen. The account continues:

> 'The British position was already precarious but appeared worse than it was...at 2000 hours the mechanised infantry of I Battalion Panzer Grenadier Regiment 192, [under Oberst Rauch] reached the sea between Lion-sur-Mer and Luc-sur-Mer a few miles to the west and linked up with the Germans [from 111 Battalion 736 Regiment] still holding out in their coastal defences.'

General Rennie responded to this armoured wedge by pulling the Hussars from Hillman, and deploying them in defensive positions on the ridgeline. He warned his tank commanders to expect a further counterattack by 21st Panzer Division.

On the other side of the Orne, Werner Kortenhaus was with *Kampfgruppe* Von Luck at St. Honorine, waiting to counterattack the weakening parachutists. With his II Battalion from the 125th Regiment already tied down in close combat with 6th Airborne Division, and after a long delay awaiting the regrouped and reassigned tanks from the panzer regiment, he launched his attack on the bridges. Assaulting from the Line of March his men could hear Von Oppeln's battle already taking place across the Orne on Periers ridge at about the same time. They made good progress until, as Hans Von Luck described it: 'All hell broke loose. The heaviest naval guns, up to 38cm in calibre, artillery, and fighter-bombers plastered us without pause. Hans was just behind his own recce advance guard and saw the disaster.

The force pulled back to dig in and contain the enemy bridgehead. von Luck recalled that at about 2100 hours they were all witnesses to what appeared to the Germans to be a lightening response to 21st Panzer Division's counter attack. This was the pre-planned fly-in of 6th Airborne Division's Air-Landing Brigade with Stirlings, Halifaxes, Dakotas and Albermarles towing Horsa and Hamilcar gliders containing the heavier weapons and equipment. 'No one who saw it will ever forget it', declared Kortenhaus, one of Von Luck's men. 'Suddenly the hollow roaring of countless airplanes and then we saw them, hundreds of them towing great gliders filling the sky.' They came down in various landing zones on both sides of the Orne, some passing directly over *Leutenant* Holler's anti-tank guns still fighting on at Bènouville against 6th Airborne Division. The sky was also filled with coloured parachutes each indicating essential supplies including ammunition for the beleaguered airborne forces astride the River. An uncanny silence seemed to descend upon everything and everyone as both sides watched in awe and consternation. Holler recollected:

We all looked up and there they were just above us. Noiselessly those giant wooden boxes sailed in over our heads to land, when men and equipment then came pouring out of them. We lay on our backs and fired and fired and fired into those gliders until we could not work the bolt of our rifles anymore. Our 2 cm flak troop shot some down and damaged many more but with such masses it seemed to make little difference.

These gliders were apparently landing behind the Germans who had now reached the coast. This caused the immediate abandonment and withdrawal of the counterattack force west of the Orne; another group of gliders landing east of the Orne bumped down directly in the path of *Kampfegruppen* Von Luck not more than 100 metres from the seventeen tanks attached from the 4th Company of the 22nd Panzer Regiment. Kortenhaus recalled:

'It was a unique opportunity, but there was a wait before the order came crackling in my earphones: 'tanks advance.' And then the air was alive with calls of: 'eagle to all, eagle to all, come in please!' engines roared into life flaps clanged shut and we rolled in cautious tempo and attack formation towards Herouvilette. But before we had even fired a shot darkness had fallen over the rolling tank formations and then warning lights shot up we were attacking positions held by our own panzer grenadiers! Baffled the men shook their heads...And that was all that we, a strong tank company, achieved on this decisive day.'

As the last gliders were landing, the Warwickshires from 185 Brigade

Oberstleutnant Hans von Luck consults a map and instructs his officers during the counter-attack against the British Bridgehead in Sword sector.

group, arrived in Bènouville to relieve the airborne forces on the Orne bridges and take over the battle with Holler's grenadiers who had been pressing hard on the canal bridge (Pegasus Bridge). In the pre-D-Day divisional plan the Warwicks should have been in Caen by now, but they were actually only half way to the city having been re-tasked in the heat of battle with a very different mission. Here they were at Bènouville having lost their Forward Observation Officer, so that they could no longer call for artillery support.

Across the very fluid and confused front line, the first tank Holler saw rolled into view opposite a house sixty metres away across a park. It halted directly in front of the muzzle of one of his 75-mm self propelled guns which was camouflaged as a large bush. But the muzzle could not be depressed sufficiently, and to start up the engine would have given their position away so the crew put their shoulders to the gun and rolled it forward. Holler described the situation:

'The suspense was dramatic but we managed it, and without being seen, either. Then Corporal Wleck cranked the gun handles frantically until the muzzle bore. Meanwhile, the English commander had got out of his turret, and walked up to the house to talk to the occupants; obviously, he hoped they would tell him where we were. As our first

shell hit, the petrol and ammunition exploded with such violence that the house beside the tank collapsed in ruins. Clearly, the English still hadn't a clue as to where we were; they fired wildly, at extreme range, and in all directions except at the 'nearest nearness', and under cover of the uproar, we were able to start up and get away.'

Consolidation

Holler cursed his lack of armoured support. Colonel Jim Eadie of the Staffordshire Yeomanry would have echoed his bitterness because at dusk his leading tanks had successfully advanced six miles from the beaches and were now at Lebisey, looking down at the divisional objective, the burning city of Caen, but without sufficient infantry support. The presence of 21st Panzer Division's two *Kampfgruppe* on his open right flank was the deciding factor, and he withdrew his force to Bieville. 'Many weeks of desperate fighting were to elapse before the regiment again stood on that high ground,' wrote a brigade historian. Similarly, Panzer Regiment 22 was reviewing the situation. The German Main Defensive Line had been ripped open by 3rd Division, the static positions of 716th Infantry Division destroyed, captured, or bypassed; there were no infantry reserves, and the tanks of the counterattack force had been ordered to dig-in and hold a defensive line instead of fighting a battle of manoeuvre.

In those few hours, the future of Caen had been decided: it had not fallen with ease – it would now be liberated over a month later, after being *martyred* or gratuitously *murdered* as some French citizens saw it. Already, many of the inhabitants had guessed the impending fate of their city and refugees now started to flee from their as yet undamaged homes. Many more would stay behind and face a more deadly outcome in the days and weeks ahead. Apart from the 200 suspected resistance workers promptly executed by the Germans in Caen prison on the morning of D-Day, many residents thought that their liberation was imminently at hand!

Meanwhile the KSLI had pushed one company forward at some cost through Beuville towards Lebisey, where it became involved in a heavy firefight, losing its company commander (Major Steel). It was then ordered to withdraw and consolidate for the night. The newly arrived enemy in Lebisey now consisted of the Panzergrenadiers of 21st Panzer Division, who were energetically digging in on the high ground north of Caen. Meanwhile the Norfolks had reached a point between Beuville and Bènouville, having suffered many casualties on the way, and the Royal Warwicks had cleared the route from St. Aubin to Bènouville and Blainville, mopping up snipers as they went. And as midnight approached the weary units of 185 Brigade dug in.

9 Brigade, on the other hand, had come ashore at 1300 hours and as Brigadier Cunningham went forward to Hermanville to contact 8 Brigade, he described the scene:

'On reaching the northern outskirts of Hermanville I was amazed to see standing inside the wall of an orchard not only General Tom Rennie but John Crocker, in their red hats. I said "I have never before been beaten into action by my divisional and corps commanders" and we had a good laugh about it. These two highly responsible and competent men realised that the moment was an extremely critical one, and they deemed it necessary to be in a position where they could give an immediate decision on any matter, perhaps affecting the whole course of the battle.

'They told me to cancel my original role of going straight down on the right to get Carpiquet and if possible Caen, and instead to get across to Pegasus Bridge to help the airborne who were hard pressed. This was disappointing, as 9 Brigade had their run down the right flank all buttoned up. However, these two officers would not have taken a major decision of that nature if they had not considered it essential. They knew that it would mean that Carpiquet would not be taken that night, unless 9 Canadian Brigade could get it alone.

'It cannot be emphasised too strongly that the commanders were on the spot to make their decision; it must have been a very hard order to give knowing what it would entail.

'My armour had not then landed, and they said I had better wait for that before moving, so on the way back to the beach I did no more than warn the KOSB that we had to get across to assist 6th airborne at Pegasus Bridge. My armour was still trying to find a place to land when I viewed it from the shore, so I returned to my brigade HQ. On arrival there, I left my carrier and went towards my armoured command vehicle. My antitank gunner and my intelligence staff moved to join me there. At that moment a stick of mortar bombs landed on us killing six and wounding six. I was wounded and unable to convey the new instructions to my staff. Colonel Dennis Orr late of the Scots Fusiliers had gone over with me as my second-in-command but between my leaving my brigade HQ and returning to it, he had been ordered to go over to Pegasus Bridge to (I think) report on the situation, certainly not to take command.

'When I was wounded he was not present to take over, and in fact I was told it was a very long time before he managed to get back. The result was a long hiatus when the brigade should have been moving and

*nothing happened. In short, if a number two is considered worthwhile,
do not use him for some other job instead.*

In the event, the Lincolns were left at Cresserons to secure the right flank with a gap remaining between the British and Canadian divisions, now being exploited by General Marcks. Meanwhile, the RUR dug in north east of Periers, while the KOSB moved across to occupy St. Aubin and the high ground overlooking Bènouville. Here, 17 Field Company RE were working furiously to build rafts and relief Bailey bridges across the Caen canal and river Orne. Sapper operations had been hampered by delays in clearing equipment from the beaches and heavy casualties, among the latter being the CRE, OC 17 Field Company, and two reconnaissance officers. Fortunately the captured bridges were held and remained intact.

So ended Rommel's *longest day*. Casualties in the Sword sector had not been as heavy as many feared, and although the immediate objective – Caen – had not been taken it had been screened to an extent. A breach five miles deep by four miles wide had been made in the Atlantic Wall by a reinforced infantry division. They had fought-off a powerful armoured counter-attack – the only cohesive response from the Germans on D-Day. As the troops wearily dug in for the night the men of 3rd Division knew that although they had accomplished much, it was only the beginning. D + 1 would soon be upon them and as Harry Jones described his feelings about that evening in his personal memoir after the war, this would be the 'longest night'.

During that first, tense night in Normandy, the enemy would be working hard to seal off the invasion area while the Allies would be adjusting plans to meet the new circumstances of a severely foreshortened beachhead. To the north of Caen the newly regrouped grenadier battalions of 21st Panzer Division were already fortifying the ridge from Lebisey to La Londe thereby dominating and protecting the approaches to Caen. Hurrying into position on their left were the fresh troops from the 12th SS *Hitler Jugend* Panzer Division. The British 3rd Division was to find these two formations an altogether different proposition from the coastal defense troops met on the foreshore on D-Day.

CHAPTER 6

FALTERING ON THE ROAD TO CAEN

The German Situation North of Caen

Dawn on 7 June found the units of 21st Panzer Division in a state of crisis. The bloodied armoured *Kampfgruppe* Oppeln was experiencing difficulties in transitioning to the defensive. There was a shortage of infantry. With a sector of five kilometers to hold, there were only two companies of infantry from I/25 Grenadier Regiment and one company of 220 Armoured Engineer Regiment available. Because 200 Anti-tank Battalion (less three guns) had been detached to the remnants of 716th Coastal Defense Division and deployed in the west of the division's sector, the tanks of 22nd Panzer Regiment had to be used as a screen to meet the next British attack.

21st Panzer Division had also lost two of its nine artillery batteries, leaving only seven batteries to cover over twelve kilometers of front. The 8th Heavy Weapons Company of 192 Regiment had pulled back from Bènouville and Blainville to a reverse slope position on the heights of Herouville near the railway bridge. At this stage there were still Germans in Beuville and Bieville. At about 0200 hours a brave German SP gun and two armoured cars slipped out of Bieville and

Sherman belonging to 13/18th Hussars.

dashed for Lebisey. They went over a necklace of seventy-five grenades placed across the road to stop enemy vehicular movement. Unfortunately the grenades failed to go off. In the Chateau de Beuville there were also sixty Germans that were cleared by Sergeant Major Lacy and gunners from the 16th Battery gun line. Rear area security was everybody's business in Normandy.

Missed Opportunities: D+1 and Beyond

The opportunity to 'bounce' Caen had been lost on D-Day and would be further relinquished on D+1. The Germans now exploited a narrow window of opportunity to first establish and then shore-up their front line north of Caen, with all the skill and urgency that the experience of four years of war had taught them. While many of the German units committed to this task were newly reconstituted or reinforced with young recruits, they still retained a cadre of professional, highly experienced tactical commanders who were able to improvise, seize the initiative, and turn any enemy weakness to their advantage. Here was a fearsome foe facing 1st Corps. It would now require a major Allied offensive to break through these positions, overwhelm the mobile armoured reserves and capture the city and its crossings over the Orne.

It could indeed be argued that 3rd Division had failed to make a concentrated thrust that might well have shattered the initially thin defensive crust offered by 21st Panzer Division. However, the dissipation of the 3rd Division's combat power by the Corps and divisional commanders, as priorities changed in the heat of battle on and shortly after D-Day, explains why Rennie was unable to complete his mission in full. As the visitor drives and walks the ground around La Londe and Lebisey, it is also clear that this highly defensible terrain favoured the German defenders. As a result, the initial attempt on D-Day by a single company of infantry with limited support from a troop of tanks had been doomed by its lack of concentrated power and fire support.

On D+1 plans were hastily made for 2 Warwicks to attack Lebisey. The battalion had already cleared Blainville at first light. Brigadier Smith, Colonel Nigel Tapp and Colonel 'Jumbo' Herdon (commanding officer 2 Warwicks) met in Blainville to prepare a simple fire plan for the attack. This single battalion attack by 3rd Division was to be mounted in confusion and with inadequate support. The stream midway between Blainville and Lebisey wood was selected as the start line. However, a basic battle drill was ignored; the start line was not secure and pockets of Germans were still around covering the valley. Captain H C Illing commanded A Company for the attack. He remembered moving forward with his Orders Group (platoon commanders and attached subordinate commanders) for a recce and having his carrier peppered with fire.

Because of delays in getting the assault force assembled Colonel Herdon postponed the attack for an hour. Unfortunately, B and C Companies were out of radio communications when this delay was imposed and they set off on time but without the preparatory barrage – the guns had received and followed the order to delay the fireplan for one hour. As the companies advanced to within 200 metres of their objective the panzergrenadiers of 125 Regiment opened fire. The attack stalled as the forward platoons were decimated, commanders killed or wounded, including Colonel Herdon, who was killed as he went forward. The Germans brought up their tanks that enfiladed the Warwicks. Into this chaos Brigadier Smith, assuming quite incorrectly that the objective had been taken, ordered forward the anti-tank guns, FOB, and carriers, still waiting in Bieville with the Warwicks Adjutant, for the order to advance and reinforce a secure objective. The column advanced up the hill as ordered. The Germans were ready for them – and still very much in control of the situation. Some vehicles got through to the other side of the wood and went into action firing back the way they had come against the Germans now closing in for the kill. Most of the vehicles and personnel were either killed or taken prisoner.

An abandoned British 6 pdr anti-tank gun and German panzer grenadiers.

A few survivors did filter back to the battalion. This was a disaster.

The Staffordshire Yeomanry had been hampered in their support role for the Warwicks attack, by the German anti-tank ditch that ran between Beauregard and Lebisey and by, as the Yeomanry War Diary for 7th June states, the 'natural anti-tank obstacle between the main axis and the road.' This natural barrier was the combination of the Dan stream bed (Le Dan Rau) that winds up from the Orne through Bieville, and le Vallon that intersects the Dan to the south of Bieville. Even today these deep watercourses remain obstacles except at their bridge sites. So without combined arms support the Warwicks attack was shattered against elements from Von Luck's I/125 Panzer Grenadier Regiment supported by tanks from 22 Panzer Regiment.

Later that day, Major Dunn recalled how Brigadier Smith had arrived at Norfolk House in the early afternoon and said to Hugh Bellamy, commanding 1 Norfolk:

> *'Hugh, I've got a bloody awful job for you; you've got to go through the Warwicks and get Stout* [codename for the Lebisey feature].

He was unable to give a situation report on the condition of the Warwicks. At 1500 Colonel Nigel Tapp was at an Orders Group at the KSLI headquarters where after some discussion the Brigadier decided to send 1 Norfolk to capture the east side of the road. Supporting fire was to be by observation as the exact whereabouts of the Warwicks was still unknown. According to Smith's own account, his order to Bellamy to restore the situation was a 'nebulous commitment.'

The Norfolks duly advanced and met heavy shell and mortar fire as well as small arms fire from the now dug-in positions of the 192 Regiment grenadiers. Despite mounting casualties they reached the edge of the wood and met up with the Warwicks. Both battalions were now pinned down and eventually the Brigadier ordered them to withdraw at 2200 hours under the covering fire of all available guns. In all two field regiments, one medium regiment, and a cruiser covered this retreat.

Illing described the withdrawal as neither coherent nor highly organised though it did prove successful. Losses in both battalions were grim. The Warwicks lost a total of ten officers and one hundred and forty other ranks as well the Anti-Tank Platoon, guns, mortars and Bren Carriers. While this tragedy was unfolding Brigadier Smith had gone forward to get some inkling of the situation only to get lost and spend the night hiding in a barn. At dawn he found his way back to his headquarters at Bieville where his Brigade Major cheered him up with a bottle of champagne.

On the other flank the CO of the KOSB had been warned early to move to Mathieu (also known to the British in 1944 as Cazelle after a small part of the village). The battalion arrived at Mathieu at 1210 hours and found it unoccupied. They then advanced down the Douvres-Caen road to Le Mesnil wood where they were ordered to gig-in much to the CO's chagrin. While still digging they were subject to heavy and accurate mortar shelling that inflicted a number of casualties. The day was brought to an uncomfortable close when they came under attack from intense small arms fire with a lot of tracer. It was a wholly unexpected attack made worse by the unmistakable sound of approaching armour. Believing the situation to be hopeless and with his position apparently surrounded, the CO ordered a withdrawal. With his piper playing 'Blue Bonnets' the battalion collected around him and made a desperate charge through the undergrowth, expecting to be met by a hail of fire as they broke from cover. As they emerged from the wood, silence fell. It was realised that the fire had come from a recce patrol from the East Riding Yeomanry

German mortar team belonging to 716 Infantry Division.

who had assumed that the battalion was a German unit! The KOSB returned to their positions somewhat embarrassed.

The Royal Ulster Rifles (RUR) also reached Le Mesnil wood at 1700 hours to reinforce the KOSB. D Company RUR and a squadron of the East Riding Yeomanry patrolled as far as Cambes but came under fire from German units. Casualties amounted to thirty-one men including two officers. A German version attaches more significance to this encounter. At 0300 on D+1 *Standartenführer* Meyer, commander of 25 SS Panzergrenadier Regiment was awaiting the arrival of his regiment at an Assembly Area on the line of Authie-St Contest-Epron. From here they were to launch a co-ordinated counter-attack at 1600 hours on 7 June with 21st Panzer Division. His troops arrived in darkness at La Folie and Couvrechef on the Caen-Douvres railway. Initial German reconnaissance indicated that the enemy did not yet occupy the villages of Carpiquet and Buron, but Villons-les-Buissons just north of Cambes had been occupied. Shortly after getting into position the SS would suffer a well-supported battalion attack against the newly arrived elements of I/25 SS Panzer Grenadier Regiment. The British attack succeeded but only after very heavy fighting and losses that prevented any further exploitation. The RUR had pushed up against the advancing elements of I/25 Panzergrenadier Regiment. The grenadiers had been supported by five tanks from 8th Company of 12 SS Panzer Regiment and by III/12 Artillery Regiment in their move towards Cambes. A violent fight had ensued, with three British tanks knocked out by German *Panzerfaust.* However, the German thrust was stopped in its tracks by concentrated artillery fire and fighter-bomber attacks. The commander of I/25 Grenadier Regiment was forced to disengage and hastily order his men to dig-in abandoning Cambes and any further prospect of an advance.

Back towards the beach, the Lincolns had temporarily been put under command of 8 Brigade while 1 Suffolk was transferred to 9 Brigade; they were told to clear the Chateau and the village of Lion. Orders had been issued at 1200 hours and a two-company attack mounted that ultimately cleared the chateau and the village but left the Germans in their strongpoint in Lion. Lieutenant Colonel Welby-Everard then issued new orders to the remainder of the Battalion to clear the strongpoint. H-Hour had been decided when new orders from brigade redirected the Lincolns to St Aubin d'Arquenay with one company to the Benouville bridges. This hasty move was conducted in trucks from the 90th Company RASC. As an indication of the urgency these vehicles were found to be still half full of petrol cans for the resupply of 27 Armoured Brigade. At Benouville they found Fox Troop of 92 Light Anti-Aircraft Regiment RA already in position and actively defending the bridges from determined German air attacks. Over a five-day period after D-Day the Luftwaffe mounted eight determined attacks in that period and seventeen aircraft were shot down by Fox Troop, 3rd Division.

The south Lancashires had also been very active. They had received orders to clear Plumetot and Cresserons after which they pushed on to Douvres-la-Deliverande. 5 Assault Regiment RE supported by the Beach Group had completed the Commandos work and cleared Ouistreham.

As a result of these efforts, the gap between 3rd Canadian and 3rd British Division was soon closed with the exception of the Douvres radar station that would not fall until 17th June. Having failed to reach the Orne in Caen on D-Day (thus gaining the security from depth and cohesion) it was essential to link up the individual beachheads as quickly as possible. 8 and 9 Brigades along with the Canadian troops, who were pressing south towards Carpiquet and Caen, were active in destroying the remaining German outposts still holding out in the gap on D+1.

These actions and the use of concentrated indirect fire, from the fleet and the army artillery assets, had spoilt the preparations for the German counter attack initially planned for 7 June. Edgar Feuchtinger (21st Panzer Division) and Kurt Meyer (commander of 12th SS *Hitler Jugend* Panzer Division's 25th Regiment) had intended to coordinate a decisive attack that would shatter the bridgehead. Meyer had rashly stated to Feuchtinger: 'Little fish! We'll throw them back into the sea in the morning.' His bravado was short lived. Feuchtinger commented afterwards:

'We decided to drive towards Douvres, and 12 SS was to take up assembly positions during the night. Artillery fire was so great that a proper co-ordination of this attack was impossible. Meyer did make a short spurt with some fifty tanks but was driven back. He never reached the start line from which our combined attack was to begin.'

The strength and intensity of Allied fire support from air, land, and sea was clearly a constant shock to the Germans and did much to shatter their attempts to

SS-*Standartenführer* Kurt Meyer.

165

fracture or destroy the expanding lodgment. Even the move up of 12th SS *Hitler Jugend* Panzer Division and Panzer Lehr had been disrupted to such an extent that they were condemned to be fed into the battle piecemeal without great gain and at serious loss.

Gains and Losses: 9 June (D+3)

On 9 June, 9 Brigade issued orders for a full-scale attack in four phases: Phase One was the capture of Cambes by the RUR; Phase Two, the capture of Galmanche by 1 Suffolk; Phase Three the capture of Malon; and Phase Four the capture of St Contest. The attack would be supported by the East Riding Yeomanry with a formidable amount of artillery fire from the Divisional Artillery and a cruiser off-shore.

The enemy in Cambes were the I/25 Panzergrenadiers that the RUR had fought over the previous two days. The II/25 had established themselves in Galmanche while the III/25 had dug in to its right north of Buron after being bloodied on the Canadians. The inter-divisional boundary between the 12th SS and 21st Panzer Division was effectively the railway line running north from Caen to Douvres and the sea. This line ran alongside the thick Norman wall around the Chateau at Cambes. The nearest troops of 21st Panzer Division to this boundary were at La Bijude on the Caen-Mathieu road and at Chateau de la Londe and Le Londel where 5 and 7 Companies of 192 Panzer Grenadier Regiment were dug-in. From La Bijude to Cambes was a clear field of fire.

The RUR started their attack at 1515 hours using a Start Line on the south edge of the village of Anisy west of Mathieu. The objective of the two leading companies was to seize the northern half of Cambes through which the follow-up companies would pass to take the rest of the village. There was some 1,500 metres of completely exposed ground from Anisy to Cambes. The battalion advanced steadily under cover of heavy supporting artillery fire. About 1,000 metres from the enemy, the advancing troops crested a small ridge and came into the full view of the Germans. The enemy now opened fire with machine guns and indirect fire. The CO of the East Riding Yeomanry was watching the RUR advance. He said, 'This is where they get to ground, and the attack is held up.'

He was wrong. The battalion continued the advance in open order. A Company on the left suffered badly losing all three of the platoon commanders and a platoon sergeant. Yet the company took its objective in the final assault. D Company, under Major Montgomery, also carried its objective. The company commander was wounded twice during this action. C Company followed up on the left and supported by five AVREs engaged the enemy beyond the village. German guns in La Bijude knocked out all five of these tanks but not before they had destroyed one panzer. There then followed five hours of vicious shelling and mortaring as the RUR consolidated. The War Diary of 9 Brigade reported that the RUR success signal was fired at 1610 hours. Radio communications were not working well but the KOSB were tasked to advance into Cambes and reinforce the RUR. At 2015 hours they advanced from Le Mesnil as far as the 8-foot wall by the railway and the grounds of the Chateau. There they assisted the RUR in clearing the village and consolidating the position. As a result of this action the RUR was awarded three MCs, a DCM, and two MM but they had lost ten officers and 172 other ranks. The KOSB had three killed and thirteen wounded in total. The losses for this operation also included Lieutenant Colonel Tom Hussey, commanding 33rd Field Regiment RA, Major Brooke commanding the direct support battery, and one of the Forward Observation Officers (Captain Roose). From 2 Middlesex, Major Passy and Captain McDowell and CSM Bell were all killed.

At about the same time that the RUR were preparing for their attack, 1 Suffolk had moved forward to an Assembly Area at Le Mesnil. The CO, Lieutenant Colonel R E Goodwin, moved forward in his carrier to be co-located with Brigade HQ ready for Phase Two. He understood that the codeword for this phase had been issued. He moved off to reconnoitre the battalion's advance to Galmache. Disaster then struck. His carrier was hit by anti-tank fire and he was severely wounded, while his Intelligence Officer and signaller were killed. Major Kit Gough, the second in command, now took over the battalion. At this point Major General Rennie came forward to assess the situation for himself and based on his analysis he gave the order to 1 Suffolk 'Firm base where you are.' The battalion established a defensive position around Le Mesnil Farm where Luftwaffe fighters, dropping fragmentation bombs, subsequently attacked them.

Major Kit Gough.

On the flanks the East Riding Yeomanry had been engaged to the west of Cambes and had two tanks destroyed while to the east, a further tank was lost to fire from La Londe. German reports of the day's actions reported the break-in to Cambes, but failed to mention the severity of their losses. The reports again emphasised the weight of enemy supporting fire but noted that this apparent attempt to split the two panzer divisions along the boundary had been foiled by the flanking support fire of 22 Panzer Regiment at La Bijude.

Stabilizing the Front

With the exception of events at Chateau de La Londe, the front from Beauregard and Herouville on the Orne Canal to Cambes in the west would be stabilised for the next fortnight. The two opposing forces now dug in, laid minefields, conducted aggressive patrolling and shelled each other. Even at this stage the campaign had already degenerated from being a battle of manoeuvre to an attritional slugging match. Both opposing armies had missed opportunities for decisive action. To some extent General Crocker had considered this eventuality in his 1st Corps Operations Order. He had stated that:

'Should the enemy forestall us at Caen and the defences prove to be strongly organised thus causing us to fail to capture it on D-Day, further direct frontal assaults which may prove costly, will not be undertaken without reference to 1 Corps. In such an event 3 Br Inf Div will contain the enemy in Caen...'

He hoped that the on-going build-up of Allied reinforcing divisions would allow for greater freedom of manoeuvre in less well-defended areas. Underlying this concept of operations was the notion the Caen was a critical pivot upon which a breakout from the western American sector of the bridgehead would swing.

The 'exception' to any change referred to above took place 10 June. According to German records the buildings of le Londel and la Londe to the north east of the Chateau de la Londe were occupied by the 5 and 7 Companies of 192 Panzer Grenadier Regiment with support from tanks at La Bijude. But during the night of the 10th D Company of the South Lancashires seized hold of Le Londel. Lieutenant Colonel Eddie Jones, then a platoon commander with the Battalion, described how the Company was able to walk in, occupy the position and begin to dig in. Some 600 metres away at the Chateau de la Londe the enemy were doing the same thing. The Battalion occupied the whole site which consisted of the Chateau le Londel surrounded with its solid stone wall, an accompanying farm house, out-buildings, and barns that made up a little hamlet on its own. The French families still in occupation were evacuated.

Chateau de la Londe – after the battles in late June.

It was an important position. From it one could see over the relatively flat ground over to Bieville to the east, Lebisey to the south east and to the high ground overlooking Caen to the south. A Company, in which Jones was serving, occupied a position on the right of the Battalion area, just forward of the farm buildings on the other side of the track that ran almost due south to the enemy positions in the Chateau de la Londe. Looking south he could see two or three knocked-out British 3-tonner trucks on the road from Mathieu to Caen. They must have driven straight into enemy lines earlier in the battle. A further attack on La Londe and the Chateau de la Londe was planned but was called off by the Brigade Commander because of signs of German reinforcement, though La Londe was still reported as clear. The Germans were clearly sensitive about holding this group of buildings that ran from La Bijude to Le Londel because that evening the enemy made preparations for an attack to re-secure the positions.

The noise of German tanks forming up was heard and a very heavy artillery barrage was opened up on them so that the attack was disrupted. The history of 21st Panzer Division states that at first light 5 Company of 192 Panzer Grenadiers, strengthened with some sappers of 220 Panzer Pioneer Battalion, was able to throw the British troops out of Le Londel and reoccupy their old positions. As Le Londel remained in British hands thereafter this German version lacks authority and is unsupported by a War Diary or other reference. Eddie Jones did describe how shelling and mortaring on Le Londel increased and at first light one morning, how a troop of German SP guns came up and began shelling his Platoon positions at point blank range for several minutes. They withdrew before any effective response could be organized. Fire was concentrated on the farm buildings instead of the slit trenches forward of them but nevertheless several of the Platoon were killed. The farm buildings were soon reduced to rubble.

The pattern of patrolling and improving defences by both sides continued for the next ten days. So did the shelling but there was a great difference. The weight of artillery fire by the 3rd Division's artillery group far exceeded that of the enemy's. German accounts draw much attention to the unceasing storm of fire they were subjected to, and the great expenditure of ammunition, which they were unable to match. In addition to supporting their own troops the 3rd Division's artillery was also kept busy in support of 6th Airborne and 51st Division across the Orne. The regular daily rate of 100 rounds per gun could be increased to as much as 400 rounds per gun during an attack.

A battery of British 155mm guns firing in support of the advance in Normandy.

To this weight of fire should be added the heavy mortars and machine guns of the Middlesex. The strength of this support was particularly encouraging to the troops confined to their slit trenches for much of the day. A 'Victor' salvo from HMS *Rodney* was also a great morale-booster. The History of 2 KSLI describes how it was the custom to fire 'One minute's worth of hate' at Lebisey several times a day with at least five regiments of guns, the fleet, all the medium machine guns, and all the mortars in range.

3rd Division learnt from a Polish deserter that this had been particularly effective on the very first attempt when it had caught the German defenders on their way to get breakfast from their field kitchen. There was a sense of grim satisfaction in the knowledge that for every shell fired at 3rd Division the enemy got at least ten back. Nevertheless, despite this disparity in the weight of shelling the Germans were still inflicting casualties. 9 Brigade suffered greatly; during the next four weeks the Lincolns reported a stream of casualties from the shelling and mortaring of their positions and as a result of the 3rd Division's aggressive patrolling policy that was enforced throughout this period.

There were some notable patrols. Captain Gilbert commanding 'C' Company 2 Lincolns moved his company out from Cambes wood to carry out a raid on known enemy positions in Galmanche to obtain, if possible, a unit identification. The plan was to form a firm base halfway between the British and German positions and then to send a strong patrol from the east and another from the west. This was done and although the enemy was initially surprised the Germans fought back fiercely. There was hand to hand fighting with many casualties inflicted on both sides. Lieutenant Pacey leading one patrol was wounded in the thigh but got back; Sergeant Ward leading the other patrol when surrounded, fought his way out with bayonet and grenade, bringing back two wounded men with him. Pacey was awarded the MC, and Ward the MM.

Lieutenant Frank Matthews with 1 Suffolk led a very successful patrol that brought back valuable information about enemy positions at La Bijude. He was severely wounded but managed to get back to his own lines. His wounds were so bad that he could not be evacuated immediately to England. On the left of the Division's line their was a similar emphasis on aggressive patrolling. The KSLI at Bieville had a thick wood known as the 'Square Wood' to their right front between Epron, the Lebisey ridge and Bieville and their own positions, which caused them some problems. It overlooked the deep ravine south of

Bieville and was a potential base of operations for enemy use. The Battalion was ordered to send out a standing patrol each night to this very dense wood. The enemy tended to mortar it quite heavily from time to time and to send out fighting patrols to dominate the area. The enemy managed to infiltrate the position on one occasion though the patrol was withdrawn successfully; a few days later a heavy mortar attack killed four and Lieutenant Higginson was so badly wounded that he died later before he could be evacuated.

185 Brigade held the left of the line from Bieville to the canal. The Norfolks had sighted a defensive line based on the south facing spur centered on the Bellevue farm complex ('Norfolk House') and the former German defensive position known in the OVERLORD operations orders as Rover. A forward screen of three platoons and the carrier platoon was sited 2,000 metres forward from the canal westwards. This was nicknamed 'Duffers Drift.' The Norfolk regimental historian gleefully noted that:

'The enemy, who obviously did not understand, motored down the road [from Herouville] *and so fell nicely in to the trap prepared by B*

Churchill AVRE.

Company. Within a week the bag was one marine officer, thirty-five other ranks, five vehicles and two motorcycles. Then someone in the enemy lines must have put up a notice to the effect that no one came back from that particular road.'

In addition to 'Duffer's Drift' the Norfolks had their share of constant patrolling. In their case this meant on the very left of the line checking the low-lying ground up to the Orne Canal that included a factory area; they also patrolled to their front towards the Lebisey position. On one of these patrols led by Captain Fearon on the forward slopes of Lebisey Wood, he and his Sergeant, were both wounded having completed their task. Fearon was unable to move and ordered Sergeant Thorne, in considerable pain himself, to return with the information. Fearon died that same day while a prisoner. On 13 June General Rennie on one of his constant visits to forward units was on his way to Cambes. The Commander of 9th Field Ambulance, Lieutenant Colonel Wood was with him and suggested a short cut. Johnnie Beck of the 3rd Recce Regiment was in Cambes as a Contact Detachment. He recorded the General's arrival in Cambes as from 'the hostile end' and the blowing up of his jeep on a British laid-mine intended to protect the position. Both the General and Colonel Wood were evacuated to England. Norman Scarfe in *Assault Division* wrote of the deep, sincere regret with which the Division heard of the General's misfortune. In the meantime Brigadier Cass took temporary command of the Division while Colonel Foster of 76th Field Regiment commanded 8th Brigade.

Mention should also be made of another action that involved part of the 3rd Division. The Radar Station at Douvres-la-Delivrande (now an excellent museum) that had been attacked unsuccessfully early on in the invasion was finally taken on 17 June. Douvres was actually a Luftwaffe strongpoint designed to protect and sustain the radar station located within its perimeter. The radar had been destroyed by air attacks about three weeks before D-Day. By 17 June the fortified installation contained about 230 men including a company of Panzergrenadiers from 21st Panzer Division and stragglers from the beach defences. Though in the Canadian sector, it was a 3rd Division team that forced the surrender of its garrison that was equipped with three Pak 5cm, three Kwk 5cm, six Flak 2cm, twenty machine guns, twelve flame throwers and three heavy and one light mortar. The commander of the strongpoint, *Oberstleutnant* Igle, held out in his position until 17 June repelling all enemy attacks. With a reinforced and buried telephone cable running from his command post to Caen he had been able to give 716th and 21st Divisions very precise target data and situation reports right up to his defeat eleven days after D-Day.

During the first few days ashore much had been happening behind the defensive positions being held by the forward infantry battalions. For the infantry there may not have been much going on the surface but nevertheless the routine was a far from relaxing one. There was stand-to at dusk and dawn. The night was occupied with sentry duties, patrols, mine laying and improving individual positions.

Feeding was an essential component of physical and mental well being for the forward combat elements. Quartermasters and their staffs did their best to ensure rations were brought up and other supplies were being delivered. It was not all as planned. The transport bringing the large packs and other essential equipment, for example cookers and food containers, for 1 Suffolk had been lost at sea in a ship that had been sunk. Though it was June the nights were still cold and the absence of greatcoats was felt. Food had to be prepared on a platoon or individual basis and it was not possible to light fires without giving away positions. The KSLI did not get their unit transportation until D+13; they should have been landed on D+4.

Throughout this period those elements not in contact with the enemy were carrying out their duties to support the forward units. Sappers, Signals, Service Corps, Medical, Ordnance, REME, Provost and that essential morale booster the Postal Unit were all working flat out, ensuring that everything that could be done in the circumstances was being done to the best of their ability. The bridgehead was still very restricted and nowhere was completely safe from shelling and bombing even though the latter was on a relatively limited scale, thus all were at risk even if they were not in the front line.

Norman Scarfe in his work *Assault Division* drew attention to the question of morale in the 3rd Division during this period. He noted that great concern had been caused amongst the troops, by the inexplicable delay in the delivery of homeward mail. No mail posted by the Division in Normandy was delivered home for over a fortnight after the assault. Even more importantly, for those serving in the bridgehead, the Press and the BBC had made absolutely no mention of the role of the 3rd Division, although other divisions such as the Canadians, the 6th Airborne and the 50th (Northumbrian) were given early coverage.

CHAPTER SEVEN

EPILOGUE: AT THE GOING DOWN OF THE SUN

The German Perspective: Rommel's 'Longest Day'

On 23 June 1944 a detailed operations report was completed under the auspices of *Oberkommando des Heeres* on the actions of 716th Division on D-Day. This report drew on surviving operations logbooks, prisoner of war reports and interviews with survivors of the many small defensive battles along the seashore and inland at the gun batteries and resistance nests; the report gives a reasonably clear indication of German perceptions of how the battle unfolded and why the Rommel doctrine failed within this divisional area of operations.

On 6 June the 716th Coastal Defense Division had been at a normal state of readiness. No reports had been received from higher command indicating that an immediate invasion in the Normandy sector was to be expected. It was not until the forward positions in 716th Division began to raise the alarm about enemy air activity, parachute landings east of the Orne, and the attack on the bridges at Bénouville (WN 13) that a full alert was ordered at 0110 hours. The report describes the response to the airborne and air-landed forces and then describes German perceptions of the seaborne assault. There is little doubt that *Generalleutnant* Wilhelm Richter was conscious of the implications of failure in Hitler's regime. He would have chosen his words carefully taking into account the risks of failure for himself and his surviving subordinates. His report emphasised material shortages such as wire, mines, labour, and concrete that had prevented the construction of defences in depth. This had left his resistance nests 'in the shape of a string of pearls'. Depth was provided by gun positions in the field of the division and by the reinforcement artillery and the communities, occupied by troops, which had been prepared for defense.'

During the early hours of the morning on 6 June General Marcks had alerted his higher Headquarters at 7th Army in Le Mans. He realized that the airborne operations being reported from the Cotentin to the River Dives east of Caen represented the initial stages of a larger, probably amphibious, operation. Thereafter, 7th Army notified Army Group B and OB West. During this critical period Rommel, was absent from his headquarters at La Roche Guyon. He was actually in Stuttgart

Generalmajor Hans Spiedel.

where he was celebrating his wife's birthday before going on to meet Hitler at Berchtesgaden on 6 June to fight his case for more resources and greater control of the Panzer arm in France. The *Generalfeldmarschall* did not learn of the invasion until 1015 hours when his Chief of Staff, *Generalmajor* Hans Spiedel – an opponent and plotter against Hitler – informed him by phone. His response was to question Spiedel as to the status of OB West's armoured reserves. Hearing that Hitler had not as yet released them, he simply stated 'How stupid of me,' and set about returning to France.

At the strategic level Adolf Hitler had responded to the news of the invasion with total assurance that his plans and preparations were complete. When his Chief of operations, General Jodl, had finally notified him of the landings he declared, with a radiant smile on his face, 'It's begun at last,' an attitude reflected in the German press. During the early hours of 6 June, Jodl had not even bothered to wake Hitler from his drug-induced sleep to present the fateful

General Alfred Jodl.

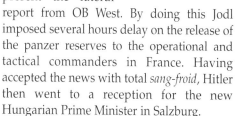

Generalfeldmarschall Erwin Rommel.

report from OB West. By doing this Jodl imposed several hours delay on the release of the panzer reserves to the operational and tactical commanders in France. Having accepted the news with total *sang-froid*, Hitler then went to a reception for the new Hungarian Prime Minister in Salzburg.

Throughout OB West the German response was confused, inappropriate and piecemeal. This was due in part to the Bodyguard operations drawing the eyes and thoughts of the German high command to the Pas de Calais. It was also due to a

combination of factors that created enormous frictions in the gears of OB West. As Carl Von Clausewitz wrote in his thesis On War over a century earlier:

'Four elements make up the climate of war: danger, physical exertion, intelligence and friction, are the elements that form the atmosphere of war and turn it into a medium that impedes activity.'

The friction referred to by Clausewitz is present in any human activity but most particularly in war. In 1944 the German high command had managed to further impede the ability of its local commanders in Normandy to make effective decisions and execute optimal plans in a timely manner. The absence of any concept of joint operations was particularly evident when the Luftwaffe and German Navy failed to co-ordinate their defensive plans and integrate their command structures with Army Group B and OB West. This weakness was highlighted when they failed to intervene in any significant manner before and during D-Day.

Even within the German land component itself there was a disunity that could only contribute to the Allied cause. Information was not passed throughout the commands as the threat emerged in the early morning of 6 June. German coastal stations had detected and reported activity at sea east of Cherbourg and north of Caen by 0250 hours yet no detailed assessment reached Corps then or later. It was not until 0900 hours that General Marcks at 84th Corps notified Army HQ that major landings were taking place. The naval bombardment being reported in the Cotentin Peninsula to Army Group B was assessed as being part of a diversionary operation. The Corps staff believed that the situation was more threatening to the north of Caen. Rommel's headquarters endorsed this analysis.

The situation in the Caen-Orne-Ouistreham sector caused much concern. Further west, at 1800 hours, the 352nd Division reported the

***Generaloberst* Friedrich Dollmann, Commander of 7th Army. Hitler would hold him responsible for the failure of the German forces to repel the invasion. He suffered a heart attack upon hearing that he was to be made the subject of an official inquiry.**

grim situation with some accuracy. Allied forces were reported infiltrating through gaps in the belt of coastal strongpoints and armour had now reached a line from Colleville, Louvieres and Asnieres. The objective of this attack was assessed as being the historic city of Bayeux. On the 352nd Division's eastern flank British forces were reported pushing inland from Le Hamel and la Riviere (Gold Beach) successfully overrunning defensive positions and threatening the Caen-Bayeux road. As a result of so much inaccurate reporting and with inadequate mobile reserves, the Germans focus of attention remained in the east of the lodgment area. Defeating the threat to Caen remained the priority.

In his 1947 post-war interview with the US Army Military History Institute while still in captivity, General Wilhelm Richter, commander 716th Division, commented on the British performance west of the Orne. He wrote:

'The choice of the divisional sector west of the Orne for attack with its very favorable terrain for landings and attack towards the south was tactically correct as well as the covering east of the Orne, in order to prevent a German attack from the east.

'The tactics of troops during the first landing were good and showed very good cooperation between all three British branches of the armed forces, based on many years preliminary practice and putting to use all combat experiences gained in Asia, Africa and Italy... The attack after the landing and the push towards the south were not launched with the same power. Despite the rapid advance of numerous enemy tanks, putting German artillery out of action, the follow-up by the infantry was, in my opinion, relatively slow.'

In a related interview in 1947, General Max Pemsel was asked to comment on Richter's statement. Pemsel responded by saying:

'The reason for the waiting attitude of the British after their great initial success, an attitude which the author [Richter] *is wondering about, was the necessity for consolidation of the wide beachhead in expectation of a German counter-attack with Panzer divisions.'*

Fortunately for 3rd Division during the early hours of the 6 June the 21st Panzer Division had been launched piecemeal towards the airborne forces astride the Orne. Later in the day, after hours of wasted effort responding to order and counter-order, two *Kampfgruppe* of the 21st Panzer Division were launched into the gap between Juno and Sword sectors north of Caen. Marcks personally supervised the attack and launched its commander, Oberst Von Oppeln-Bronikowski, into battle with his now famous, if dire warning: 'Oppeln, if you don't succeed in throwing the British into the sea, we shall have lost the war.'

The assault was quickly smashed against an exceptionally well-sited 3rd Division anti-tank screen and a perfectly positioned armoured regiment in support, on the high ground from Beuville northwards along the Periers Ridge.

The next days would be characterized by an increasingly desperate attempt to bring up the 1st SS Panzer Corps and mount a co-ordinated armoured counter-attack in the Caen sector. As the German land line communications, network collapsed under air, naval bombardment  and resistance operations radio communications increased allowing the Ultra organization at Bletchley Park to take a more active role in monitoring and identifying the move of the critical reserves towards Normandy.

In the days following D-Day one of Ultra's most significant contributions to the success of NEPTUNE-OVERLORD was the identification of Headquarters Panzer Group West at a critical moment when it was about to co-ordinate a significant armoured thrust at the beachheads. In a near perfect example of a reconnaissance-strike operation, Geyr Von Schweppenburg's command group was detected, recognized and identified and

General Geyr von Schweppenburg

within hours attacked by Mitchell bombers and rocket firing Typhoons. At 0920 hours on 11 June the telephone log at German 7th Army Headquarters recorded:

> 'G-3 [probably 7th Army] informs G-3 Army Group B that...the Panzer Group West has been knocked out by a direct hit on its Headquarters. Command has been give to the First [SS] Panzer Corps.'

D-Day in Review

At the end of D-Day the 1st British Corps was ashore, short of its objectives, but ashore. In truth none of the OVERLORD assault divisions had achieved their missions in full, however, they had all successfully breached Hitler's *Festung Europa*. The Allies had executed a complex plan with its many interdependent and intricate parts. They had also landed a substantial force with such effect that the Germans would not be able to dislodge them. Each side now rushed to build up

General Sir Bernard Montgomery.

forces and materiel in Normandy in order to establish a cohesive front line. However, in the forthcoming days the Allies and the Germans would both miss opportunities for decisive action and so condemn their armies to a grueling war of attrition that would last well into August.

The Operational commander, Montgomery, had a clear idea of the next phase of the campaign. So before looking at the achievements of D-Day in isolation, consider Montgomery's evolving concept of operations for his subsequent planned breakout. After the initial disruption and setbacks on and after D-Day, a change of plan was necessary. In simple terms Montgomery decided to use the Allied beachhead like a door, which, hinged on the eastern end with Caen as the pivot in 3rd Division's sector, would swing open increasingly wider from the west. To achieve this he had to lure the majority of the German divisions, and in particular the panzer divisions, east to face the British 2nd Army, thereby making it easier for the American First Army to break out in the west. The battles you may see further evidence of, during your visit to Normandy at Avranches, Mortain, and Falaise, form a part of the evolving concept.

The Americans were to take Cherbourg and then break out south, west and then finally east. And this is essentially what happened. For planning purposes Montgomery hoped to reach the river Seine by D+90. In the event the Americans reached the river on D+75, thanks to several weeks of grinding, costly attrition and then the relatively successful Allied encirclement operation, which culminated to the south of Falaise – all-be it inconclusively.

Consider the achievements of D-Day. Working from west to east. On the extreme west the two American airborne divisions had a pretty chaotic time. Their flight-path, coming in from the north-west carried them across the Cherbourg peninsula, here they met both thick cloud and flak. Jumping at 0130 hours, the 101st Airborne Division was scattered widely. By dawn, only 1,100 men of the 6,600 had reached their rendezvous. Jumping an hour later at 0230 hours, 82nd Airborne Division fared little better. Elements of one battalion quickly secured the vital junction at Ste. Mère Église after a small but bloody battle for the town; however, much of the rest of the division was liberally scattered across the flooded areas, and in particular only a few of the gliders, with the heavy weapons and equipment, arrived on target. Thanks to the skill and courage of small groups of isolated American paratroopers most missions were accomplished against what on the face of it appeared overwhelming odds. These two divisions certainly confused the Germans about what was going on and helped to dissipate German responses that would otherwise have further hampered the landings at Utah and Omaha.

On Utah beach the 4th US Division actually fared well. A strong tide and an error in navigation forced them to land 2,000 metres south of their original objective, but this did not matter. By midday they had advanced across the narrow causeways (secured by the airborne forces) about four miles inland and linked-up with major elements of 101st Airborne Division.

The story of Omaha beach is very different. Launched some eleven miles out as a result of inflexible naval commanders adhering to the letter of the plan, the landing craft had a difficult run-in through heavy seas. They arrived on the beach having lost almost all their DD Tanks, which had drowned, to find that the gently sloping beach of some 3-400 metres was overlooked by undamaged and fully manned defensive positions on the bluffs that were about 80-100 feet above the seashore. And that bluff was bristling with fresh, experienced German infantry in well-prepared positions. Pinned-down on the beach under heavy fire for several hours the initial assault floundered and almost failed. At one stage Bradley had considered pulling the survivors off Omaha and abandoning this landing in favour of Utah. As a result if inaccurate situation reports from Bradley's headquarters, Eisenhower actually ordered a

General Omar Bradley

USAAF bombing strike along the beach that would have done even greater damage to the hapless assault divisions. This catastrophe was

181

averted when it turned out that no aircraft were available in England. Only by mid to late morning could the Americans break through the crust in any strength onto the bluff thanks ultimately to the individual courage of a number of tactical leaders and some timely naval gunfire support from Destroyer Squadron 18. By the end of the day the 1st and 29th Divisions had advanced about two to three miles, having formed a very small and very vulnerable beachhead. There is no doubt that the prospect of conducting an opposed landing at Omaha Beach even today would not appeal to any soldier or marine.

In the British sector H-Hour on Gold Beach was 0725 hours, nearly an hour later than the Americans. This was because of the different tide states along the coast. This time difference also allowed the British to have a two-hour preparatory naval bombardment. In the event this was of benefit. 50th Division was a highly experienced division. It had fought in North Africa and taken part in the Sicily and Italian landings. It fared well; fighting a series of seemingly isolated actions at battalion and company-squadron level it was seven miles inland by the end of D-Day – the furthest of all assault divisions, and only one mile from its objective. Although it must be recorded here that the 4/7th Dragoon Guards, a cavalry regiment equipped with Shermans, actually reached its objective (the Caen-Bayeux road) on D-Day only to be withdrawn on orders.

The story of the Canadians on Juno is not dissimilar. After initial hard fighting they overcame the beach defences and advanced between five and six miles inland. An important objective was Carpiquet airport, west of Caen, which they failed to achieve on D-Day. Subsequently, due to the ferocious defence mounted there by the *Hitler Jugend*, Carpiquet would not be taken until early July.

Still further east, 3rd British Division landed at Sword. Most witnesses agree that 3rd Division had the most ambitious task of all – to capture or mask the city of Caen. Its achievements were disrupted by enemy action, the challenges created by a narrow frontage for the beach assault, and difficulties getting inland from that overcrowded beach area. With the notable exception of a single battalion, 3rd Division was impeded by powerful defensive positions, the need to support the 6th Airborne Division astride the Orne, and in responding to an armoured counter-attack by 21st Panzer Division. The static positions might have been brushed aside or bypassed more quickly under different formation commanders or a more manoeuvre-based doctrine. However, one of a number of exceptional achievements within the divisional area was made by 2 KSLI, which set out to capture Caen alone, and got to within two to three miles of the city. But unsupported, and faced with elements of 21st Panzer Division, they could get no further.

To the east of 3rd Division, the 6th Airborne Division was attempting, and for the most part succeeding, to secure vital targets in the area of the Orne valley, and east of it towards the River Dives.

Yet what of the Germans? For the static infantry divisions there was little option but to fight where they were. After all, they had only limited tactical mobility ranging from horse-drawn transport and bicycles to flat feet. The only formations capable of mobile, offensive operations were the three armoured divisions: 21st Panzer Division under Rommel's direct command, and the two others, Panzer Lehr and 12th SS Panzer Division, all suffering from a complex and confused chain of command culminating at the top with Hitler.

It is also worth briefly considering the quality of the opposing troops. When studying the Normandy campaign the reader may identify something of the different outlooks of the Allied divisions engaged. For example, there is no doubt that the 7th British Armoured Division, the famous 'Desert Rats', was never the fighting force in Normandy that it had been in the desert. And the same is true of the almost equally famous and battle-experienced 51st Highland Division.

On the German side 21st Panzer Division had been the key division in Rommel's great Afrika Korps. But after its extraordinary successes in the desert, it had been pushed back to Tunisia, where large elements of it had been destroyed or forced to surrender. Reconstituted for the Normandy campaign it never achieved its earlier standards; yet it was the only armoured division available to Rommel on that critical day. Panzer Lehr and 12th SS *Hitler Jugend* Panzer Divisions were very different. While the former was certainly an excellent division, 12th SS *Hitler Jugend* Panzer Division was clearly outstanding. Its name – *Hitler Jugend* – suggests why this was. It was formed of

SS-*Brigadeführer* Fritz Witt.

those young men who in the 1930s and early 1940s had been members of Hitler's fanatical youth movement. The excellent divisional

Young men of the crack Division, 12th SS _Hitler Jugend_ Division. Devoted to their Führer.

commander, general Fritz Witt was killed on D+5, only to be succeeded by the remarkable General Kurt (Panzer) Meyer, a veteran of 31 years of age. Under his command, the _Hitler Jugend_ division would excel itself wherever it appeared on the battlefield for the rest of the war.

The Führer Adolf Hitler.

If Rommel had been allowed to launch these two excellent divisions on D-Day things might have looked very different but Hitler had frozen them, and no-one dared to wake the Führer on the morning of 6 June to ask for their release. Much of the German High Command had also been transfixed by the outstanding deception plan focusing attention on the Pas de Calais. It is worth remembering that to many German senior officers Normandy was a diversionary attack. So Rommel, or rather Spiedel, his Chief of Staff, since the Field Marshall was now in transit back from his leave, only had the 21st Panzer Division available with its centre of mass actually south of Caen. As a result of order, counter order, and disorder, it only attempted decisive action in the invasion area in the mid-afternoon and then in three dispersed columns. Ordered to attack astride the Orne and drive the British into the sea, it lacked a clear main effort. This made it vulnerable to the ambushes and hasty defence of 3rd Division. East of the Orne it had met 6th Airborne Division during the night of 5/6 June and made little headway, despite the fact that it possessed tanks while the airborne forces were scattered and weak in comparison.

West of the Orne the panzers had succeeded in halting the almost unsupported advance by 2 KSLI on Caen and then drove on north through the gap between the Canadian and British beachheads. It even reached the sea, but its brief moment of victory evaporated and turned to dismay when the grenadiers saw the massed follow-up gliders of 6th Airborne Division fly-in and land behind them.

By the time Rommel reached his HQ at la Roche Guyon at 2200 hours on the night of 6 June, after a hectic drive from Germany, the chances of defeating the invasion on the beaches had gone. By the end of D-Day well over 130,000 Allied troops were ashore – NEPTUNE had succeeded – two out of three of Mountbatten's prerequisites for victory laid down in 1941 had been met and a tenuous foothold in northwest Europe had been seized.

3rd Division's Operations in Retrospect

Finally, and before leaving Sword sector recall the graves in Hermanville's immaculately maintained CWGC Cemetery; ponder the sacrifice of so many young men. Imagine their fear and sense of duty as they approached the hostile shore on that cold, wet Tuesday

Men of HQ 9 Brigade on D-Day.

morning on 6 June 1944. Many of them never reached Caen thirty-four days later – their D-Day objective. They were cut down in their assault craft, or under the guns of the fearsome beach strongpoints at Cod, Trout, or inland at Hillman. Many would fall victim to German direct and indirect fire during the brutal fighting inland at Lebisey and at La Londe. Their youth, courage, *esprit de corps* and their fear remain constants of any effective army in any conflict.

Today the last surviving veterans of the Iron Division in Normandy recall the events of half a century ago with startling clarity and great pride. Their memories of the first hours on the beach and the fighting inland amongst the villages, fields and lanes are still crisp and clear, etched on their minds. Many of these venerable gentlemen even now recount their impressions with emotion.

On Omaha Beach, fifty years after D-Day, President William Jefferson Clinton of the United States spoke these words that apply to all the Allied servicemen and women who fought to liberate Europe from the evil totalitarian regime of Adolf Hitler:

> *'On these beaches the forces of freedom turned the tide of the 20th century...let us not forget that when they were young, these men saved the World'*

Remember them.

ORDER OF BATTLE:
3RD BRITISH DIVISION ON SWORD BEACH

8 INFANTRY BRIGADE (ASSAULT BRIGADE)

1st Battalion The Suffolk Regiment
2nd Battalion The East Yorkshire Regiment
1st Battalion The South Lancashire Regiment

185 INFANTRY BRIGADE (FOLLOW UP BRIGADE)

2nd Battalion The Royal Warwickshire Regiment
1st Battalion The Royal Norfolk Regiment
2nd Battalion The King's Shropshire Light Infantry

9 INFANTRY BRIGADE (RESERVE BRIGADE)

2nd Battalion The Lincolnshire Regiment
1st Battalion The King's Own Scottish Borderers
2nd Battalion The Royal Ulster Rifles

DIVISIONAL TROOPS

HQ 3rd Division
3rd Recce Regiment RAC
7th, 33rd and 76th Field Regiments, RA
20th Anti-Tank Regiment RA
17th, 246th and 253rd Field Companies, RE
2nd Battalion The Middlesex Regiment (MG)

UNITS UNDER COMMAND FOR ASSAULT PHASE

27TH ARMOURED BRIGADE
13/18th Royal Hussars
The Staffordshire Yeomanry
The East Riding Yeomanry

1 (SPECIAL SERVICE) BRIGADE

3, 4 and 6 Commandos
45 (RM) commando
2 Troops 10 (RA) Commando (French)
1 Troop RM Engineer Commando

Extracts from Lieutenant Colonel Welby-Everard's address to the 2nd Battalion, Lincolnshire Regiment, prior to D-Day.

COMMANDING OFFICER'S ADDRESS TO THE BATTLION - SAT 27 MAY 44

"The last time I spoke to you up at HAWICK I told you that I would be talking to you again before we went overseas, and that is what I am going to do now. I have got a certain amount of things I want to say, but I won't keep you longer than I can help. We have had rather a long time waiting for what we are about to do, and it is disclosing no secrets to say that that period of waiting is nearly over, and therefore I want to take this opportunity - probably the last one I shall have for some time - of talking to you altogether and making certain points to you.

Now, first of all, the general points regarding the coming operations. The most important thing, I think, is to get it in its true perspective. Don't consider it as just one operation that this particular army, to which we belong, is taking part, because it isn't that at all. It is merely a part of very much larger operations that are taking place all over the world, and in other places in EUROPE from the place to which we are going ourselves. And you can look upon it as the final - and I am quite sure it is going to be the final - thrust at Hitler which is going to come to him from every direction from which we can possibly do it, simoultaneously.

When you are briefed, as you will be on Monday, and you see maps and photographs, have a really good look at them so that you get a picture in your mind of the sort of country that you are going to. Some of these photographs are absolutely first class - most of them are - and it really will be in your own interests to have a jolly good look at them. You will see pictures of the beaches and pictures of some of the things that the Hun has put up on the beaches. Well, if you see what they are like - and you will see what they are like because they are extremely good photographs - you won't be surprised when you actually see the real things.

The next point is one that you have been told time and time again during training exercises. Your Officers and your NCOs always shout at you "Don't Bunch" Well now, that is a thing with which one gets rather fed up of being told during training, but it is, and will be, a very important point indded, and the Div Comd has said himself that he thinks that in the open no soldier should ever be less than 7 to 10 yards away from another one. That is quite a long distance when you come to think of it. So don't after, say, an attack, or after some operation or manouevre that you have been doing - don't get into a little bunch of four or five, because if a shell does come it will hit all five of you instead of the one wretched, unfortinate person who happens to be there.

The second essential is one that we have all heard of, and that has been drummed into you in your training the whole time. That is the offensive spirit. We have got to be absolutelt slap out for getting the initiative and keeping it, and that can only be done by really studied and determined effensive tactics.

Thirdly, - the third point is enthusiasm. I talked about those four first days which are going to be exhausting and probably absolute hell. We have got to get into the right frame of mind to tackle it. Well now, if one really feels that we are all going to do a really good job, then it is much easier to go on, but no army was ever successful unless it really meant to get there.

Fourthly is confidence - confidence in the team, that is, the Allied Team, the Battalion and confidence in ourselves. Confidence that we know our job and we are going to do it well, and better than the chap the other side. And lastly, is really very much the same one as I have just talked about - going hard and keeping at it, oming the natural exhaustion.

Now, I will just give you these five again, and think over them hard :-

        Allied co-operation.

        The Offensive spirit.

        Enthusiasm.

        Confidence and,

        The will and determination to go on.

SOME RECOMMENDED MUSEUMS

Bayeux. MUSEE DE LA BATAILLE DE NORMANDIE, Boulevard Fabian Ware (Tel: 02 31 92 93 41), provides an excellent overview of the Battle for Normandy up to the closure of the Falaise Pocket in August 1944. A thirty-minute film is shown in French and English (admission fee).

Across the street is the Commonwealth War Graves Commission Cemetery (CWGC) containing 4,868 graves. This is the largest British Second World War cemetery in France. Opposite the entrance, is the Memorial to the 1,837 missing British soldiers from the Normandy campaign.

While in Bayeux it is worth visiting the Centre Guillaume le Conquerant (admission fee) and viewing the Bayeux Tapestry on rue de Nesmond (Tel: 02 31 51 25 50).

Arromanches. THE MUSEE DU DEBARQUEMENT (Tel: 02 31 22 34 31) is located on the promenade in the center of town (admission fee). From this museum and the cliffs above (to the east) the visitor will have excellent views and explanations of the Mulberry Harbor complex, still visible offshore over half a century after its construction to protect Port Winston.

Arromanches. THE CINEMA CIRCULAIRE (Tel: 02 31 22 30 30) at Arromanches is located on the cliff top above the town. It offers a dramatic 360-degree impression of the liberation. There is an entrance fee; varied showing times.

Caen. The Memorial: UN MUSEE POUR LA PAIX (Tel: 02 31 06 06 44) inaugurated in 1988 on the site of a German fortified HQ. There is an entrance fee and it is open from 0900-1900 hours daily. The museum has only limited exhibits but provides a dramatic audio-visual display of the war, the battle for Normandy, and the liberation. There is a substantial research facility (including multimedia), restaurant, a child's play area, park, and an excellent bookshop. The Museum can be reached on www.unicaen.fr/memorial or memorial@unicaen.fr.

Ouistreham: Resort town and port, Calvados département, Basse-Normandie région, northwestern France. Situated at the mouth of the Orne River, it is nine miles (14 kilometres) northeast of Caen to which it is linked by road, the Orne River, and the ship canal. Ouistreham's Romanesque and Gothic church was built in the 12th and 13th centuries. The town was a prominent regional port until the construction in the 19th century of the ship canal to Caen. Some port activities continue, including yachting, fishing, and ferry services, the latter linking the town to Portsmouth, England with an excellent Brittany Ferries service. Adjoining Ouistreham to the west on the English Channel coast is the smaller resort town of Riva-Bella, where the 4TH COMMANDO MUSEUM (also known as the SWORD BEACH MUSEUM) commemorates the D-Day (June 6, 1944) landing of British and French Commandos.

The Great Bunker of Riva-Bella is a German-built coastal artillery command and control centre that now houses a museum focusing on the Atlantic Wall (Tel: 02 31 97 28 69) system of German coastal defences . It contains a collection of documents and relics and gives an excellent view of the mouth of the Orne.

Port en Bessin: The MUSEUM DES EPAVES SOUS MARINES DU DEBARQUEMENT (D-Day Wrecks: 02 31 21 17 06). This is a remarkable collection of salvaged wrecks from inshore sites where vehicles and paraphernalia of NEPTUNE-OVERLORD were lost during the battle for the lodgment. Located between Bayeux and one kilometre south of Port en Bessin.

Douvre la Deliverande: MUSEE RADAR DOUVRES (Tel: 02 31 37 74 43). This unique museum is devoted to the 'Secret War' of radar. It is sited in two remarkably renovated German bunkers in the former German radar site and garrison.

WHERE TO STAY

The Normandy Tourist Board offers an excellent service. The Board's offices can provide lists of recommended hotels, campsites, 'gites' and 'chambre d'hote' and having ascertained your preferences will make the booking for you for a small administrative fee. Convenient offices can be found in:

Bayeux: pont St. Jean on the corner between St. Jean and rue Larcher. Tel: 02 31 92 92 40.
Caen: pl. St. Pierre by the Eglise St. Pierre. Tel: 02 31 27 14 14.
Carentan: to the left of the Mairie (Town Hall). Tel: 02 33 42 74 01.
French Government Tourist Offices are located in London and New York:
London: 178 Piccadilly, London W1V 0AL. Tel: 0171 629 1272.
New York: 444 Madison Ave., 16th fl., New York, NY 10022. Tel: (212) 439 1400.
The Normandy Tourist Office also has an office in the UK:
The Old Bakery, Bath Hill, Keynsham, Bristol BS31 1HG
Tel: 0117 986 0386   http://www.Normandy-tourism.org.

INDEX